"A Long Time Coming"

"A Long Time Coming"

THE INSPIRING, COMBATIVE 2008 CAMPAIGN AND THE HISTORIC ELECTION OF BARACK OBAMA

Evan Thomas

WITH EXCLUSIVE,
BEHIND-THE-SCENES REPORTING
BY THE STAFF OF

Newsweek.

PublicAffairs

New York

Published in the United States by PublicAffairs™,
a member of the Perseus Books Group.

Book Design by Jane Raese

Library of Congress Cataloging-in-Publication Data
Thomas, Evan, 1951–
A long time coming : the inspiring, combative 2008 campaign and the historic election of Barack Obama / Evan Thomas ; with exclusive, behind-the-scenes reporting by the staff of Newsweek. — 1st ed.
p. cm.
ISBN 978-1-58648-607-5 (hardcover)
1. Presidents—United States—Election—2008. 2. Political campaigns—United States. 3. Obama, Barack. I. Newsweek. II. Title.
JK5262008 .T56 2009
324.973'0931—dc22
2008051492

First Edition

10 9 8 7 6 5 4 3 2 1

CONTENTS

U.S. President-elect Barack Obama stands onstage along with his wife Michelle and daughters Malia (red dress) and Sasha (black dress) in Grant Park on November 4, 2008, in Chicago, Illinois. Obama defeated Senator John McCain by a wide margin in the election to become the first African-American U.S. president-elect.

PROLOGUE

The Age of Obama

Jon Meacham

H E WAS, ONCE, the consummate outsider. The first time Barack Obama saw the White House was a quarter century ago, in 1984, when he was working as a community organizer based at the Harlem campus of the City College of New York. President Reagan was proposing reductions in student aid. The young Obama, just out of Columbia, got together with student leaders—"most of them black, Puerto Rican, or of Eastern European descent, almost all of them the first in their families to attend college"—to take petitions protesting the cuts to the New York delegation on Capitol Hill. Afterward, Obama wrote in *The Audacity of Hope*, the group wandered down Pennsylvania Avenue to the Washington Monument and then to the White House, where they stood outside the gates, looking in.

The glib literary move at this point would be to note how Obama, who will become the forty-fourth president of the

United States on Jan. 20, 2009, will now return to that house to undo the work that was unfolding inside all those years ago—the work of the Republican Party of Nixon, Reagan and George W. Bush. But the story, like Obama himself, is more complicated than one might think. The Democratic Party's success in 2008 is not a straightforward revenge-of-the-left drama. Many true believers say this is the dawn of a new progressive era, a time of resurgent (and in many ways rethought) liberalism. The highly caffeinated have high hopes. At the same time, many conservatives—most, it seems, with a show on Fox News Channel—see things the same way, and believe an Age of Obama will be a grim hour of redistribution at home and weakness abroad.

But if Obama governs as he ran—from the center—then there will be disappointed liberals and conservatives. The left may feel somehow cheated, and the right, eager to launch perpetual assaults on the new administration, could well find Obama as elusive and frustrating as the opposition found Reagan.

Parallels from the past risk seeming irrelevant and antique given the enormity of the historical moment. A nation whose Constitution enshrined slavery has elected an African-American president within living memory of days when blacks were denied fundamental human rights—including the right to vote. Hyperbole around elections comes easy and cheap, but this is a moment—a year—when even superlatives cannot capture the magnitude of the change that the country voted for on November 4, 2008. "If there is anyone out there who doubts that America is a place where all things are possible; who still wonders if the dream of our Founders is alive in our time; who still questions the power of our democracy, tonight is your answer," Obama told an adoring yet serious throng in Chicago's Grant Park on the night of his election. He alluded to the historic nature of the victory only indirectly. "This election had many firsts and many stories that will be told for generations," he said. He did not need, really, to add anything to that: that he was saying the words was testament enough.

Obama ran, in part, by arguing that his candidacy tran-scended race. Perhaps it did; many of us believed that his skin color, unusual name and unfamiliar background might well cost him the election. As it turned out, he won deci-sively, a rare feat for a Democratic presidential nominee. Does this mean that America is now beyond black and white? No, but we are much further ahead than we were a year ago. Obama's victory, no matter what one's politics, is a redemptive moment in the life of a nation for which race has been called, simply and starkly, "the American dilemma."

John McCain is a man of honor, a patriot who has lived a life of service and devotion to country. He was, however, on the wrong side of history in 2008. Like Hillary Clinton, also a formidable American and public servant, he had the great personal misfortune to be standing in the path of an un-stoppable political force. (One of the riddles of the age will be what might have happened had he survived the South Carolina primary in 2000 and defeated Bush for the Repub-lican nomination eight years ago.) External forces, chiefly the economic collapse in the autumn and President Bush's stubbornly low approval ratings, created an environment that made a GOP victory virtually impossible. With a man of Obama's undeniable political gifts on the other side, the task became actually impossible.

Like Franklin D. Roosevelt in 1932 and Reagan in 1980, the Obama win of 2008 marks a real shift in real time. It is early yet, but it is not difficult to imagine that we will, for years to come, think of American politics in terms of Before Obama and After Obama. Certainly many of his voters already see the world this way. Exit polls suggest that one of every 10 voters was casting a ballot for the first time, and they were overwhelmingly minority or young. Eighteen- to 24-year-olds accounted for roughly the same percentage of the electorate—17 percent—as they did in 2004, but while the split four years ago was 54–40 percent for John Kerry, it was 68–30 percent for Obama, a net swing of 24 points in Obama's favor, which was by far the biggest shift in any age group.

Their battles are not the battles of their fathers and mothers. Why, Obama once asked someone he identified only as "an old Washington hand," did the capital of the first decade of the 21st century feel so much harsher than the postwar era? "It's generational," the man replied. "Back then, almost everybody with any power in Washington had served in World War II. We might've fought like cats and dogs on issues. A lot of us came from different backgrounds, different neighborhoods, different political philosophies. But with the war, we all had something in common. That shared experience developed a certain trust and respect. It helped to work through our differences and get things done." That version of the past was heavily edited: Joe McCarthy was a veteran, too.

Still, the point stands. Shared experiences tend to create shared values. Even the epic events of recent years—September 11, Iraq, the economic crisis—cannot begin to give the Obama coalition anything like World War II to smooth the rough edges of partisanship. His voters share convictions, not experiences. Chief among these convictions is a passion for a change from the rule of George W. Bush and an unabashed love for Barack Obama.

In this light, Obama has more in common with Reagan than appearances might suggest. Reagan's loyalists believed in his issues, or at least one of his issues, and they believed in him. They were anxious for a change from the incumbent administration at a time of shattered confidence and economic turmoil. The comparison is revealing, for it may foreshadow the nature of the next four or eight years. Like Reagan, Obama is an astute performer, a maker of myths and a teller of stories. Like Reagan, he is popularly seen, by friend and foe alike, as an ideological purist—but has demonstrated a tendency toward the pragmatic. Like Reagan, he is the leader of a core of believers so convinced he is on their side that they are likely to forgive him his compromises.

Obama gets the Gipper. "Reagan spoke to America's longing for order," he has written, "our need to believe that we are not simply subject to blind, impersonal forces but that we can shape our individual and collective destinies, so long as we rediscover the traditional virtues of hard work, patriotism, personal responsibility, optimism and faith."

A man with a vivid literary and historical imagination, Obama is something of a dreamer, if a down-to-earth one. As a senator, he saw things that are not there, but once were. "Sometimes, standing there in the chamber, I can imagine Paul Douglas or Hubert Humphrey at one of these desks, urging yet again the adoption of civil-rights legislation; or Joe McCarthy, a few desks over, thumbing through lists, preparing to name names; or LBJ prowling the aisles, grabbing lapels and gathering votes. Sometimes I will wander over to the desk where Daniel Webster once sat and imagine him rising before the packed gallery and his colleagues, his eyes blazing as he thunderously defends the Union against the forces of secession."

Visiting the White House when he arrived in Washington as a senator, Obama mused: "The inside of the White House doesn't have the luminous quality that you might expect from TV or film; it seems well kept but worn, a big old house that one imagines might be a bit drafty on cold winter nights. Still, as I stood in the foyer and let my eyes wander down the corridors, it was impossible to forget the history that had been made there—John and Bobby Kennedy huddling over the Cuban missile crisis; FDR making last-minute changes to a radio address; Lincoln alone, pacing the halls and shouldering the weight of a nation."

It is telling that his visions ended before the middle of the 1960s, a decade that has disproportionately shaped subsequent decades. Obama's campaign was about moving beyond the wars of the baby-boom generation. In this he is a contradictory figure. Pressing a centrist message in the presidential campaign, he had a reliably liberal and not terribly interesting voting record in the Senate. Which Obama will show up for work in the White House? The New New Democrat, or the safely liberal former community organizer from Chicago? It seems safe to say that he would not have won as he did if he had appeared to be an eloquent Walter Mondale, or a tactically brilliant Michael Dukakis. He ran as a more practical kind of center-left politician—not a Great Society liberal, but one who, in the tradition of Bill Clinton, believes in pursuing progressive goals through centrist means and with an occasionally conservative cultural message. The "socialist" attacks of the McCain-Palin ticket failed in part because they stretched credulity.

Liberals who have thrilled to Obama could grow disenchanted with him if he fails to deliver a progressive Valhalla by, say, Valentine's Day. But the Reagan example offers a different—and more likely—possibility. Given Obama's popularity with his base, he may be that rare politician who can get away with making a deal without being seen as selling out. Reagan raised taxes and nobody held it against him, or even noticed all that much. Obama could be a Teflon man for the new century.

One thing is certain: Obama knows the Washington game he disdains, and he knows it well. He confounded virtually every prognostication in the campaign, and he knows politics, psychology and history. He understands that patience is a rare American virtue, and that it is easy to lose one's perspective. "When Democrats rush up to me at events and insist that we live in the worst of political times, that a creeping fascism is closing its grip around our throats, I may mention the internment of Japanese Americans under FDR, the Alien and Sedition Acts under John Adams, or a hundred years of lynching under several dozen administrations as having been possibly worse, and suggest that we all take a deep breath," he wrote.

Before the crowd in Grant Park, Obama acknowledged the difficulties: "two wars, a planet in peril, the worst financial crisis in a century." In characteristically serious tones, he downplayed expectations, trying an all-too-novel approach in American politics: he was (basically) honest about what awaits us. "The road ahead will be long," he said. "Our climb will be steep. We may not get there in one year or even one term, but America, I have never been more hopeful than I am tonight that we will get there." But he quickly came back to earth. "There will be setbacks and false starts," he said, promising that "I will always be honest with you about the challenges we face."

To govern well, Obama will need all those spirits he once evoked—FDR, Kennedy, Lincoln—and he will need an understanding public. Two years ago, on the eve of his campaign for president, Obama said this about the American people: "I imagine they are waiting for a politics with the maturity to balance idealism and realism, to distinguish between what can and cannot be compromised, to admit the possibility that the other side might sometimes have a point."

Now he has the chance to help make such a politics a reality. On the night before the election, en route from Akron, Ohio, home to Chicago, Obama wandered back into the press section of his campaign plane, thanking reporters—especially those who had been with him from the beginning. "It will be fun to see how the story ends," said Obama, as he headed to the front of the plane. Yes, Mr. President-elect, it will.

With ANDREW ROMANO

Senator Obama talks with his senior staff—David Axelrod (left) and Robert Gibbs (right)—backstage before speaking to supporters at a town hall meeting in Erie, Pennsylvania, on April 18, 2008. Senator Hillary Clinton won the Pennsylvania primary vote four days later.

Photo by Charles Ommanney / *Newsweek*

ONE

How He Did It

Sometimes, Barack Obama wondered whether
he really was "the One," as Oprah called him.
But Hillary Clinton's campaign was chaotic.

BARACK OBAMA HAD A GIFT, and he knew it. He had a way of making very smart, very accomplished people feel virtuous just by wanting to help Barack Obama. It had happened at Harvard Law School in the mid-1980s, at a time when the school was embroiled in fights over political correctness. He had won one of the truly plum prizes of overachievement at Harvard: he had been voted president of the law review, the first African-American ever so honored. Though his politics were conventionally (if not stridently) liberal, even the conservatives voted for him. Obama was a good listener, attentive and empathetic, and his powerful mind could turn disjointed screeds into reasoned consensus, but his appeal lay in something deeper. He was a black man who had moved beyond racial politics and narrowly defined interest groups. He seemed indifferent to, if not scornful of, the politics of identity and grievance. He showed no sense of entitlement or resentment. Obama had a way of transcending ambition, though he himself was ambitious as hell. In the grasping race for status and achievement—a competition that can seem like blood lust at a place like Harvard—Obama could make hypersuccessful meritocrats pause and remember a time (part mythical perhaps, but still beckoning) when service to others was more important than serving oneself.

Gregory Craig, a lawyer in Washington, D.C., was one of those Americans who wanted to believe again. Craig was not exactly an ordinary citizen—he had served and worked with the powerful all his life, as an aide to Sen. Edward Kennedy in the 1980s, as chief of policy planning at the State Department in the Clinton administration and as a lawyer hired to represent President Clinton at his impeachment trial in the U.S. Senate in 1999. He had seen the imperfections of the mighty, up close and personal, and by and large accepted human frailty. But, like a lot of Americans, he was tired of partisan bickering and yearned for someone who could rise above politics as usual. A 63-year-old baby boomer, Craig wanted to recapture the youthful idealism that he had experienced as a student at Harvard in the 1960s and later at Yale Law School, where his friends included Bill Clinton and Hillary Rodham. In the late fall of 2003, he was invited to hear a young state senator from Illinois who was running for the U.S. Senate. Craig was immediately taken with Barack Obama. "He spoke 20 to 30 minutes, and I found him to be funny, smart and very knowledgeable for a state senator," Craig recalled.

Craig was so visibly impressed that his host that evening, the longtime Washington mover and shaker Vernon Jordan, teased him, saying, "Greg has just fallen in love."

IT WAS TRUE. CRAIG READ Obama's book *The Audacity of Hope*, which, Craig said, "floored me," and later chanced to ride with Obama on the Washington shuttle. He read Obama's earlier autobiography, *Dreams of My Father*, and was "blown away," he recalled. "In my judgment, he showed more insight and maturity than Bill Clinton at the age of 60 in terms of understanding himself." In November 2005, Craig sat next to George Stevens, an old friend of the Robert Kennedy clan, at another Obama speech. Stevens leaned over to Craig and said, "What do you think of this guy for president? I haven't heard anybody like this since Bobby Kennedy." Craig instantly replied, "Sign me up." Stevens and Craig approached Obama coming out of the speech and asked, "What are you doing in 2008?" Obama gave them a big grin and said, "Oh, man, it wasn't *that* good." But before long Craig and Stevens were raising money for Obama's political-action committee, the Hope Fund. Obama was amused by the devotion of the two old Kennedy hands. After a while, every time he saw the two men he would say, "Here come the Kool-Aid boys."

In December 2006, Obama told Craig and Stevens, "Lay off me for a while. I've got to talk to Michelle." Obama went off to Hawaii with his wife and two girls for the holidays. "I thought, 'We're dead,'" recalled Craig. "He's not going to be able to do it."

Craig was not wrong to be pessimistic. Obama could marshal a lawyerly set of arguments about how he could win, that the country was at a "defining point" and that Obama was the best hope to bring change. "I, I, I actually believe my own rhetoric," Obama stammered, uncharacteristically, in an interview with *Newsweek* in the spring of 2008. But Michelle was not eager to subject her family to a process that was dangerous and ugly—uplifting and history making, maybe, but also a potential family wrecker. Her kids would be given cute names by the Secret Service ("Radiance" and "Rosebud," as it turned out), but their lives would never be the same.

Obama had been warned. In November 2006, at dinner at a fancy Italian restaurant in Washington, former Senate majority leader Tom Daschle had reminded Obama that he had never really been attacked before. "I told him he should think about how he might react if his wife was attacked—the emotional discipline it takes," recalled Daschle. At about the same time, with his fellow Illinois senator, Richard Durbin, Obama had talked about the physical risks. At a political event at the Union League Club in Chicago before Thanksgiving, Obama told Durbin that many of his African-American friends were advising him not to run, some of them because they were afraid he would get killed. (Durbin shared their fears and began lobbying to get Obama put under Secret Service protection. In May, eight months before the first primary, the Secret Service would begin standing watch over Obama, the first time such protection had been extended to a candidate so early in the process.)

Michelle Obama was worried about her husband's safety, but was also seized with a kind of free-floating anxiety, recalled Durbin. Even after she said yes, she asked Durbin, "They're not setting him up, are they?" The "they" was all the people who were urging Obama to run. Michelle wondered at their motives.

Obama understood his wife's fears and even, to some degree, shared them, but he had a way of turning empathy into persuasion. "Her initial instinct was to say no," Obama recalled. "She knew how difficult it was for me to be away from the girls, she feels lonely when I'm not around, so her initial instinct was not to do it. And I think she also felt that, you know, the Clintons are tough, and that I would be subject to a lot of attacks." So that Christmas season, Michelle and Barack went for some long walks on the beach in Hawaii, where they were visiting his grandmother, and "just talked it through. It wasn't as if it was a slam-dunk for me," said Obama. "I think part of the reason she agreed to do it was because she knew that she had veto power, that she and the girls ultimately mattered more than my own ambitions in this process, and if she said no we would be OK." Michelle was able to extract a promise: if he ran, her husband would have to quit smoking.

In some ways, running for president was a preposterous idea for someone who had served as a two-term state legislator and had spent only two years in the United States Senate. But Obama, a careful student of his own unique journey, could see the stars coming into alignment—the country was exhausted by the Iraq War (which he, alone among leading candidates, had opposed as "dumb" from the outset). As Obama saw it, the conservative tide in America was ebbing, and voters were turning away from the Republican Party. People were sick of politicians of the standard variety and yearned for someone new—truly new and different. Another politician with a superb sense of timing, Bill Clinton, perfectly understood why Obama saw a golden, possibly once-in-a-lifetime, opportunity. The former president believed that the mainstream press, whose liberal guilt Clinton understood and had exploited from time to time, would act as Obama's personal chauffeur on the long journey ahead. "If somebody pulled up a Rolls-Royce to me and said, 'Get in,'" Clinton liked to say, with admiration and maybe a little envy, "I'd get in it, too."

BARACK OBAMA CAN BE COCKY about his star power. On the eve of his speech to the Democratic convention in 2004, the speech that effectively launched him as the party's hope of the future, he took a walk down a street in Boston with his friend Marty Nesbitt. A growing crowd followed them. "Man, you're like a rock star," Nesbitt said to Obama. "He looked at me," Nesbitt recalled in a story he liked to tell reporters, "and said, 'Marty, you think it's bad today, wait until tomorrow.' And I said, 'What do you mean?' And he said, 'My speech is pretty good.'"

Obama's 2004 convention speech launched him into the strange world of celebritydom; he acquired the kind of aura that can transform a skinny, scholarly man with big ears into a sex symbol. Eureka Gilkey, one of Obama's aides, recalled going with him when he made a speech to the Democratic National Committee shortly after he began his campaign. Obama was mobbed outside the bathroom. "These were DNC members; they're supposed to be jaded by politicians," recalled Gilkey. "Not trying to tear their shirts off. I remember going home that night, and my boyfriend saying, 'What is that purple bruise on your back?' I had bruises on my back from people pushing and shoving, trying to get to [Obama] . . . I remember grabbing women's hands because they were trying to pull his shirt from his pants. I couldn't believe it."

Obama was growing accustomed to adulation. Greg Craig was not the only old Kennedy hand to fall in love. At Coretta Scott King's funeral in early 2006, Ethel Kennedy, the widow of Robert Kennedy, leaned over to him and whispered, "The torch is being passed to you." "A chill went up my spine," Obama told an aide. The funeral, he said, was "pretty intimidating."

Obama understood that he had become a giant screen upon which Americans projected their hopes and fears, dreams and frustrations. Maybe such a person never really existed, couldn't exist, but people wanted a savior nonetheless. As a bestselling memoirist he had created a mythic figure, a man named Barack Obama who had searched and quested and overcome travails, who had found an identity and a calling in public service. Obama recalled that he often joked with his team, "This Barack Obama sounds like a great guy. Now I'm not sure that I am Barack Obama, right?" He added, pointedly, "It wasn't entirely a joke."

In the first quarter of 2007, Obama put the political world on notice when he raised $24.8 million, more money than any other Democrat, and drew huge crowds at his early rallies. But he was a tentative, awkward presence in the endless Democratic debates through the spring and summer of 2007. He didn't really seem to have his heart in it; he appeared to lack the required, almost pathological drive to be president. The campaign strategist, David Axelrod, told Obama he worried that the candidate was "too normal" to run a presidential campaign, and Obama began wondering himself. He missed going to the movies and reading a book and playing with his kids. He worried about "losing touch" with "what matters." To a *Newsweek* reporter he said, "I'm not trying to say that I'm some sort of reluctant candidate—obviously this is a choice I made. But there was some tension there in my own mind." He seemed so distracted in one debate that one of his rivals, former senator John Edwards, came up to him during a break and scolded him, "Barack . . . you've got to *focus.*"

Obama bridled at the sometimes mindless rituals and one-upmanship of a national political campaign in the age of cable news. He resented the pressure he felt to declare, as he put it to *Newsweek*, that you "want to bomb the hell out of someone" to show toughness on terrorism. He was surprised when Hillary Clinton refused to shake his hand on the Senate floor after he declared his candidacy. And he was upset with his own campaign after a low-level staffer referred in a press release to Clinton as "(D-Punjab)" because of her ties to supporters of India. "I don't want you guys freelancing and, quote, *protecting me* from what you're doing," he lectured his staff. "I'm saying this loud and clear—no winks, no nods here," he said, irritated to take the heat for a clumsy dirty trick he had not known about and would never have authorized. "I'm looking at every one of you. If you think you're close to the line, the answer isn't to protect me—the answer is to *ask* me."

Obama was something unusual in a politician: genuinely self-aware. In late May 2007, he had stumbled through a couple of early debates and was feeling uncertain about what he called his "uneven" performance. "Part of it is psychological," he told his aides. "I'm still wrapping my head around *doing this* in a way that I think the other candidates just aren't. There's a certain ambivalence in my character that I like about myself. It's part of what makes me a good writer, you know? It's not necessarily useful in a presidential campaign."

These candid remarks were taped at a debate-prep session at a law firm in Washington. The tape of Obama's back-and-forth with his advisers, provided to *Newsweek* by an attendee, is a remarkably frank and revealing record of what the candidate was really thinking when he took the stage with his opponents.

On the tape, after Obama's rueful remark about the mixed blessings of his detached nature, there is cross talk and laughter, and then Axelrod cracks, "You can save that for your next memoir."

Obama continues: "When you have to be cheerful all the time and try to perform and act like [*the tape is unclear;*

Obama appears to be poking fun at his opponents], I'm sure that some of it has to do with nerves or anxiety and not having done this before, I'm sure. And in my own head, you know, there's—I don't consider this to be a good format for me, which makes me more cautious. When you're going into something thinking, 'This is not my best' . . . I often find myself trapped by the questions and thinking to myself, 'You know, this is a stupid question, but let me . . . answer it.' Instead of being appropriately [*the tape is garbled*]. So when Brian Williams is asking me about what's a personal thing that you've done [that's green], and I say, you know, 'Well, I planted a bunch of trees.' And he says, 'I'm talking about *personal.*' What I'm thinking in my head is, 'Well, the truth is, Brian, we can't solve global warming because I f—ing changed light bulbs in my house. It's because of something collective.'"

Obama was refreshingly honest with his aides, who chuckled over his remarks, but he was no Happy Warrior, and his detachment deflated his staff a bit. His campaign headquarters at 233 North Michigan Avenue in Chicago was high tech—lots of flat screens, more cell phones than regular phones—but earnest and nerdy. (A large hand-lettered sign stuck on the bathroom door instructed staffers to BRING BACK HOTEL SHAMPOOS AND SOAPS FOR DONATIONS TO SHELTERS.) A former Clinton staffer, accustomed to the earthy chaos of the Clinton war room (where, in legend at least, James Carville refused to change his lucky underwear), found it a little soulless. A newcomer to the campaign in September 2007, Betsy Myers—sister of former

Clinton press secretary Dee Dee Myers and a former Clinton White House staffer herself—hoped that Obama, in town overnight, might come to headquarters to cheer the staff. "But he didn't," she recalled later that fall. "He went to the gym instead." She paused as she recollected. "He hasn't been in the headquarters in months. A lot of these people are young and really look up to him, and it would have meant a lot to them if he'd stopped by." Another pause. "Nobody would have had to tell Bill Clinton to stop by if he was just a couple of blocks away. You would have had to physically *drag* Bill Clinton out of there."

THE LOW POINT, OBAMA LATER recalled, came in September and October, when he trailed Clinton in the national polls by 20 to 30 points. His staff was complaining that he lacked "energy." But Obama wasn't that worried. He trusted his chief strategist, Axelrod, a former newspaperman with a melancholy look, an ironic air and a clear sense of what to do: make the campaign about change, and make Hillary Clinton out to be more of the same. A veteran of numerous state, local and national campaigns, Axelrod, at 52, was an idealist who liked to read old Bobby Kennedy speeches in his spare time but who was well versed in gut-cutting politics, Chicago style. Axelrod had suffered in his own life (his father committed suicide; one of his children was severely epileptic), and he kept a certain detachment. He was courtly and gentle, not at all the more typical hit-'em-again macho political consultant. He liked Obama in part because he could see that the candidate was unusually intelligent (especially, in his experience, for a politician coming out of the Illinois State-house), and because Obama seemed uninterested in and unimpressed by the mindless tit-for-tat of modern political campaigning. Axelrod was, like Obama, self-contained. He did not use an office at the gleaming high-tech headquarters but rather worked from his own low-key office and spent much of his time at a greasy deli called Manny's. Axelrod was a seer and a good listener, though not much for glad-handing and schmoozing.

To run things, Obama counted on David Plouffe, who was calm and a little nerdy himself. (Staffers joked that Plouffe's range of emotions ran all the way "from A to B.") Plouffe reflected the cool self-discipline of the candidate, and the two of them set the ethos of the campaign, which staffers dubbed "No-Drama Obama." Plouffe also had a clear and simple plan: concentrate on four early states—Iowa, New Hampshire, Nevada and South Carolina. Clinton might be ahead in the national polls, but Obama knew he was raising record amounts of money—and, even better, in small amounts over the Internet, which meant that donors would not get tapped out. The campaign had 37 field offices in Iowa. No other campaign was so well organized.

Obama had laid out his vision for the campaign on the day after the midterm elections in 2006. The Democrats had routed the Republicans in Congress, and Obama sensed that the moment had arrived for an unconventional campaign that would take advantage of voter disenchantment—not just with the Republicans but with politics as usual. He had met in a small, dimly lit conference room in the office of Axelrod's consulting firm in Chicago with his inner circle: Michelle, his friend Marty Nesbitt, Axelrod, Plouffe, Robert Gibbs (who would handle communications), Steve Hildebrand (Plouffe's deputy), Alyssa Mastromonaco (director of the advance teams) and Pete Rouse, Tom Daschle's former chief of staff and a Capitol Hill insider. Valerie Jarrett, a close Obama family friend who was closely connected with Chicago Mayor Richard M. Daley, joked about the decidedly unfancy setting. There were cookies, bottled water and canned soda—"whatever kind of pop you wanted," Jarrett said with a laugh as she later recounted the scene. "This is David Axelrod."

Obama spoke first. "I just remember him saying that if he were to do this, he wanted to make sure that it was a different kind of campaign and consistent with his philosophy of ground up rather than top down," Jarrett recalled. As a community organizer in Chicago in the '80s, Obama had been influenced by the teachings of Saul Alinsky, a radical with a realist bent who once wrote, "Any revolutionary change must be preceded by a passive, affirmative, non-challenging attitude toward change among the mass of our people." Obama knew he had a knack for finding nonthreatening ways to make people accept change—to begin with, his own skin color. As Jarrett recalled, Obama insisted that he wanted to run a grass-roots campaign because he had seen it work as a community organizer, and he wanted to try to take the model and go national. Rouse, the old Washington hand, had a slightly different recollection of the meeting: the grass-roots model wasn't really a choice. It was a necessity. Hillary Clinton would have the establishment behind her, which meant that she'd have the early money (or so it was thought), the endorsements and a national organization.

For the meeting, Rouse had prepared a list of six questions. The third question was: "Are you intimidated about being the leader of the free world?" Obama had a ready answer: "Who wouldn't be?"

Thus, in a dim room in Chicago, was launched one of the most formidable political operations ever seen in American politics. But its potential was not obvious at the time. Obama fretted about his showing in the early going, particularly his shaky debating skills. "It's worse than I thought," he told Axelrod after he watched the videotape of one dismal performance in the summer of 2007. But he felt he was learning on the stump—at his own pace and in his own way. Obama was a relentless self-improver—"I'm my own worst critic," he told *Newsweek*—but he was also a loner who needed to step back away from the others, to look more closely at himself. He wasn't chilly, exactly, but for a politician he was astonishingly inner-directed, and that could make him seem remote. He felt a little overprotected by his handlers, who would signal from the back of the hall that he had time for only one or two questions from the public— and none from the press. Obama began ignoring the signal from Gibbs, his communications director, instead taking three or four more questions from the crowd, though he still kept his distance from reporters. (Curiously, though Obama drove his rivals mad by receiving reams of mostly friendly publicity, he was not well liked by reporters, many of whom found him chilly and guarded. He was more popular with editors, who regarded him as a phenomenon.)

On the stump, he decided to experiment, to try loosening up a little. Speaking to an African-American crowd in Manning, S.C., on Nov. 2, he began to riff, using the call-and-response cadence of a black preacher. Addressing the doubts among some blacks about whether the country was ready to vote for an African-American, Obama said, "I just want y'all to be clear . . . I would not be running if I weren't confident I was gon' win!"

There was a rousing chorus of "Amen!" and cheers from the audience.

"I'm not interested in *second* place!" More cheers, and a big grin from Obama . . . he could feel the crowd's energy.

"I'm not running to be *vice* president! I'm not running to be *secretary* of something-or-other!" They were like old friends now, Obama and the crowd . . . this was fun!

But then Obama got carried away with himself and violated a cardinal rule of braggadocio in the black community: don't get too high and mighty.

"I was doing just *fine* before I started running for president! I'm a United States senator *already!*"

In an instant the crowd went quiet—and that should have been his cue . . . but Obama plowed ahead.

"Everybody already *knows* me!" A lone shout went up from the audience.

"I already *sold* a lot of books! I don't *need* to run for president to get on television or on the radio . . ."

Silence.

"I've *been* on Oprah!" That seemed to get the crowd back, but Obama knew he had almost lost them altogether.

OBAMA STUDIED HIMSELF AND learned, just in time. The annual Jefferson-Jackson Day Dinner in Des Moines on Nov. 10 was a crucial beauty pageant before the real contest, the caucuses on Jan. 3. Obama's Iowa organization made sure to pack the hall and drown out the supporters of all the other candidates. Because the candidates were not allowed to use teleprompters, Obama spent hours memorizing the words and perfecting his delivery. The speech was a good one, ripping George W. Bush and taking down Hillary (a little more subtly), and it built into a crescendo as Obama told the story of how, on a miserable morning when he faced a small, bored crowd in Greenwood, S.C., a single black woman in the audience had revived his flagging spirit by getting the crowd to chant, responsively, "Fired up!" "Ready to go!" Slipping from an easy, bemused tone to a near shout, Obama egged on the overflow crowd at the J-J dinner. "So I've got one thing to ask you. Are you FIRED UP? Are you READY TO GO? FIRED UP! READY TO GO!" *The Washington Post's* David Broder, the Yoda of political reporters, was watching and understood that Obama had found the Force. The speech became Obama's standard stump speech, and in the weeks ahead it never failed him. Broder described the effect of Obama's thumping windup: "And then, as the shouting became almost too loud to hear, he adds the five words that capsulize the whole message and send the voters scrambling back into their winter coats and streaming out the door: 'Let's go change the world.' And he sounds as if he means it. In every audience I have seen," Broder reported on Dec. 23, a week and a half before the Iowa caucuses, "there is a jolt of pure electrical energy at those closing words. Tears stain some cheeks—and some people look a little thunderstruck."

For someone who had reportedly coveted the White House for years, who had long plotted with her husband to take back the presidency and restore the Clinton imperium, Hillary Clinton was slow to actually declare for the nomination. "We utterly squandered '05 and '06 in terms of her running for president," recalled one Clinton adviser. For someone who was known as a fierce battler, who was in fact courageous in adversity, she was oddly detached and conflict-averse as a boss. There were moments when it seemed she wasn't all that eager to give up her solid, useful life as a U.S. senator to pursue the Clinton destiny, at least as it was understood by the press and by the former president. On a cold midmorning in January 2007, Hillary sat in the sunny living room of her house on Whitehaven Street in Washington, a well-to-do enclave off Embassy Row where she lived with her mother and, on occasion, her husband. She was finishing a last round of policy prep with her aides before getting on a plane to Iowa for her first big campaign swing. In a moment of quiet, she looked around the living room and said, to no one in particular, "I so love this house. Why am I doing this?"

Her policy director, Neera Tanden, and her advertising director, Mandy Grunwald, laughed, a little too lightheartedly. Clinton went on. "I'm so comfortable here. Why am I doing this?"

Tanden spoke up. "The White House isn't so bad," she said.

"I've been there," said Clinton.

For most of her political life, and for most of the campaign to come, Hillary Clinton was a stubborn fighter. She was a very able lawmaker; indeed, she was more dutiful and effective in the Senate than Obama was. But she was, to a degree not generally recognized at the time, not a strong manager. She was unable to control her own staffers, who from the very first skirmish with the Obama forces showed questionable judgment and mutual distrust.

In late February 2007, Maureen Dowd of *The New York Times* ran a much-noticed column, an interview with David Geffen, a big-time Hollywood producer. Hollywood money had always flowed into the Clinton coffers, but Geffen had just given a big fundraiser for Obama. Geffen explained why, using code that anyone could understand: "I don't think that anybody believes that in the last six years, all of a sudden Bill Clinton has become a different person."

To say that Geffen's remark struck a raw nerve in the Clinton camp is a mild understatement. "We're just praying that Bill behaves," a Clinton staffer told a *Newsweek* reporter that winter. She clasped her hands and bowed several times. Other staffers dryly referred to the private plane owned by supermarket magnate and playboy Ron Burkle, Bill Clinton's friend and traveling buddy, as "Air F——One."

Geffen's remarks to Dowd, which were sure to ricochet around the political world by lunch, presented the Clinton war room with its first real challenge. Howard Wolfson, Hillary's bulldog spokesman, had read the column by 5 A.M., called her by 6 and summoned a crisis conference call by 7. By the time most Americans were arriving at work, Wolfson had put out a statement calling on Obama to denounce Geffen's statement and return the money from the fundraiser. The Obama war room responded with a not-so-subtle crack about selling the Lincoln Bedroom in the Bill Clinton administration. The Clintonites were delighted—as they saw it, the Obama team had taken the bait and fallen into a trap. Wolfson issued a press release: "OBAMA EMBRACES SLASH & BURN POLITICS: By refusing to disavow the personal attacks . . ." It was an all-hands-on-deck moment, with every staffer in the Clinton war room on the phone with a reporter, pushing the story.

It was exciting. Combat! First blood! But lost in all the frantic Googling, Nexising and IMing was the larger picture. By overreacting, the Clinton campaigners drew attention to their own misgivings about the former president's behavior and to Obama's status as a legitimate contender who could raise big bucks from the Clintons' own base. Obama himself floated coolly over the whole flap, telling a reporter, "It's not clear to me why I should be apologizing for someone else's remarks. My sense is that Mr. Geffen may have differences with the Clintons, but that doesn't really have anything to do with our campaign."

Before too long, reality set in among Clinton's staffers, and the finger-pointing began. According to other staffers,

Mark Penn, Hillary's prickly chief strategist, had been all for the assault on Obama, but when he saw it backfiring he told Bill Clinton that he had not been involved, that it was Wolfson's fault. With Hillary Clinton, he suggested that perhaps Wolfson, who was cast in the press as a hit man out of *The Sopranos*, wasn't up to the job of chief spokesman in a presidential campaign. For good measure he took a swipe at Grunwald, officially the campaign's chief ad person, though Penn regarded himself as the campaign's true image maker. "You have to fix this," said Hillary. Penn nodded. "We have to make him think that he's in charge of communications," Penn said conspiratorially, "the same way we made Mandy think she's in charge of ads."(Penn later denied this account.)

The story, while byzantine, was a perfect microcosm of the campaign to come: a Hollywood mogul uses a famous columnist to revive old rumors of the candidate's husband's infidelities; the candidate's campaign panics and ends up aggravating the problem; the campaign's chief strategist washes his hands of the whole situation, and when the candidate tells him to "fix it" he sees an opportunity to undermine two other top staffers—without fixing anything.

Crisis, chaos, deceit and subterfuge. After eight years in the Clinton White House, it was all familiar to Hillary—a world she had bravely struggled in but not against; it was the only world she really knew.

The Clinton campaign blew through cash: fancy hotels like the Bellagio in Las Vegas and the Four Seasons everywhere; thousands of dollars on flowers and valet parking;

and one memorable $100,000 grocery bill at a Des Moines supermarket. Hillary never spent a night in a motel in rural Iowa if she could possibly avoid it. She preferred to overnight in the Presidential Suite in the Des Moines Embassy Suites and to fly alone in private jets, without the press or staff. Her campaign manager was her former White House scheduler, Patti Solis Doyle, who had coined the term "Hillaryland" to describe the circle of women loyalists around Hillary and referred to Bill's circle of advisers as "the White Boys." Chief White Boy was Penn, who, during the dark days of 1994, had come into the Clinton White House with Dick Morris, the secretive and now shunned former adviser. Penn and Solis Doyle barely spoke. More important, Penn, who was in charge of polling data, shared his findings with Bill Clinton—but often kept them from Solis Doyle and the other advisers (who naturally assumed he was hiding any results that didn't jibe with his strategy).

Penn especially did not get along with Harold Ickes, a top aide from the White House days. The two men were a volatile match. Penn's social skills were limited; Paul Begala, another old Clinton hand, privately joked that Penn had Asperger's syndrome, because he was narrowly smart and generally clueless. Ickes was a labor lawyer with a spectacularly foul mouth, even by campaign standards. By midwinter, an account of Penn and Ickes screaming the F word at each other would make it into *The Washington Post*. Campaign manager Solis Doyle seemed overwhelmed by it all. Her door was often closed, and she sometimes did not return phone calls. The *New Republic* reported campaign gossip that she was inside her office watching soap operas. (Actually, she was answering e-mails until the early hours of the morning.)

T HE CAMPAIGN SEEMED TO LURCH from message to message, in part because Penn wanted to go negative against Obama, and Solis Doyle, Wolfson, Grunwald and Ickes wanted to "humanize" Hillary. "She's not going to go around talking about *feelings*," Penn would sneer. Solis Doyle, who liked nicknames and acronyms, dubbed Penn "the Chairman of the Kill Him Caucus." Hillary was unable to choose between the two approaches. Ads attacking Obama or softening Clinton were made—and then put on the shelf while her advisers bickered. Hillary's lame first campaign slogan, designed by default and by committee, was "I'm in It to Win." ("No s——," Ickes muttered to a *Newsweek* reporter.)

Clinton liked to describe her campaign as a "team of rivals," borrowing from the title Doris Kearns Goodwin used for her book on Abraham Lincoln and his strong-willed and disputatious, but ultimately triumphant, Civil War cabinet. A top adviser may have more accurately captured the spirit of the Clinton campaign when remarking to a *Newsweek* reporter, "It was a terribly unpleasant place to work. You had seven people on a morning call, all of whom had tried to get someone else on the call fired, or knew someone on the call tried to get them fired. It was not a recipe for cohesive team building."

Throughout the fall of 2007, Clinton was hailed as "inevitable" by a good portion of the press corps. Even so, her campaign was suffused with a sense of grievance—that Obama was getting a free ride and that reporters were itching for her or her husband to trip up. At a debate in Philadelphia in late October, Hillary, looking sick and exhausted, stumbled on a question after parrying with her opponents for more than an hour. Asked whether she supported New York Gov. Eliot Spitzer's plan to allow illegal immigrants to apply for driver's licenses, she answered yes, no, maybe. Sen. Chris Dodd, then John Edwards, pounced. The Clinton campaign posted a video it dubbed "Piling On," a rapid-fire montage of the men onstage attacking Hillary in the debate. The press accused her of playing the victim, which just heightened the sense among the Clintonites that she was a victim—of a double standard that judged women more harshly than men, especially one particular black man. The feeling deepened a couple of weeks later when Obama, at another debate, botched the same question on immigration and went unscathed by the press.

The Clintonites were not entirely wrong about the press. At the final Iowa debate, on Dec. 13, Obama was asked how he could really present himself as the candidate of change when so many of his advisers had worked in the Clinton administration. As he professorially cleared his throat ("Well, you know, I . . . "), a sharp laugh erupted from Hillary, who exclaimed, "I want to hear this!" Obama allowed himself a bit of drollery, remarking, "Well, Hillary, I'm looking forward to you advising me as well." Reporters watching in the press area began debating whether Clinton's laugh was really a "cackle" and cracking jokes about "Cruella de Hil."

Obama was starting to feel confident, even cocky again. During December, he took Oprah Winfrey with him as a kind of warmup act, and crowds by the tens of thousands began turning out in the early-winter chill. Winfrey spoke of reading *The Autobiography of Miss Jane Pittman*, how the enslaved Pittman was searching for "the One," the child savior who would lead her people to freedom. "Well, I believe, in '08, I have found the answer to Ms. Pittman's question. I have *fo-o-u-und* the answer! It is the same question that our nation is asking: 'Are you the one? Are you the one?' I'm here to tell y'all, he is the one. He is the one . . . *Barack Obama*!!" Waiting backstage, Obama peered out at the crowd of 30,000 and did a little dance with Michelle. At a huge rally with Winfrey in South Carolina, Obama cast off his habitual reserve and shouted so loud his voice cracked. "I just want to know, ARE YOU FIRED UP? READY TO GO! F-I-I-RED UP? READY TO GO!! F-I-I-REDUPREADYTOGOFIRED-UPREADYTOGOFIREDUP READYTOGO . . ." again and again, until Stevie Wonder came blasting from the speakers: "Here I am-m-m-m ba-a-a-by, signed, sealed, delivered, I-I-I'm yo-o-o-u-u-urs!!!"

Obama was not given to shows of emotion. But at the last debate he was asked an innocuous question about his New Year's resolution, and he launched into standard-issue boilerplate about being "a better father, better husband. And I want to remind myself constantly that this is not about me, ah, what I'm doing today. It's an enormous strain on the family . . . a-a-a-nd . . ." He paused, and for the briefest moment there was a hitch in his voice before he continued, "Y'know, yesterday I went and bought a Christmas tree with my girls, and we had about two hours before I had to fly back to Washington to vote . . ." Valerie Jarrett, the family friend who had become one of his closest political advisers, thought Obama was going to tear up. She had seen it before, at a book party for *The Audacity of Hope* in 2006, when Obama had started to say he was sorry to have been away from his family so much during his campaign for the Senate, and began crying so hard he couldn't go on. Obama was remarkably self-contained, but he was also palpably emotionally attached to his family. Jarrett knew that he had not been able to keep his promises to Michelle about getting home to see her and the kids, and that the strain was starting to show.

At 6 P.M. on Jan. 3, 2008, the night of the Iowa caucuses, Obama, Jarrett and Plouffe drove to one of the canvass locations, a large high school in Des Moines. The parking lot was packed. The three of them just looked at each other, Jarrett recalled. The crowd, mostly white, many wearing Obama T shirts, swirled around them. Obama thanked a young Asian boy for coming out to vote—it was his first election—and when Obama turned away, Jarrett noticed that there were tears streaming down the boy's face. Obama seemed reasonably relaxed to Jarrett. He went off to dinner, but his staff didn't pay him much attention. Their heads were all lowered as they peered at their BlackBerrys, looking for early voting returns.

Over at Clinton headquarters, the preternaturally optimistic Terry McAuliffe, a longtime Clinton fundraiser, thought his candidate would win by 10 points. Nearly everyone had told him so, though Penn, holding close the polls, had hedged with a lot of caveats and footnotes. (Penn later said that the senior staff had access to his polls and that he issued no turnout estimates.) At 8 P.M. McAuliffe stood in the middle of the campaign boiler room and boomed, "How are we doing?" Wolfson, the spokesman, walked by on the way to get a piece of pizza. "We're getting killed," said Wolfson. "We're going to get killed. We're going to get our asses kicked."

The Clintonites had vastly underestimated the turnout. Penn had originally figured 90,000 Iowans would turn out on a snowy night (the pollster/strategist later boosted the number to 150,000). On the night of Jan. 3, 250,000 came to stand around in crowded gyms and be herded into preference groups for one candidate or another. Some 22 percent were under the age of 25, an unusually high percentage from an age group not known for voting. Hillary won just 5 percent of their votes.

An aide approached McAuliffe and said the president wanted to see him. McAuliffe was escorted to the Clintons' suite by a Secret Service agent. He found Bill Clinton watching a bowl game on TV. The ex-president seemed perfectly relaxed and jovial. "Sir," said McAuliffe, "have you heard the news?" "What news?" Clinton asked. "We're going to get killed," said McAuliffe.

"What!" exclaimed Clinton, who then called out in a loud voice, "Hillary!"

Hillary emerged from the bedroom. McAuliffe recalled: "Nobody had told them. He thought he was going to have a beer with me and watch the game." Suddenly there was pandemonium. Grunwald and Penn appeared, then Solis Doyle and Wolfson and Neera Tanden, the policy director. "How did this happen?" the Clintons demanded. A squabble broke out when Grunwald showed some negative ads on her laptop that had been made—but never aired. Penn insisted that the argument—that Obama had overstated his antiwar credentials—had tested well; it was the ads themselves, made by Grunwald, that were no good. Now President Clinton wanted to run the ads. "Let's go," he said, giving a thumbs-up. But Hillary asked, "Where are we going? It's just throwing stuff against the wall."

The plane flight back to Manchester after midnight was grim. "Mark, we lost *women*," McAuliffe said. Penn just shrugged his shoulders. At a senior staff teleconference in the morning, Hillary, who had slept no more than an hour, asked for ideas. There was an awkward silence. So she held for a bit, then asked for input. Again, silence. "Well, I want to thank you all," she said. "It's been really great talking to myself." Then she hung up.

Less than 24 hours before the New Hampshire polls opened on Tuesday, Jan. 8, she was sitting in a strip-mall coffee shop in Manchester, talking to about 16 voters, when someone asked, "My question is very personal: How do you do it? How do you do . . . how do you keep upbeat and so wonderful?" Hillary answered, "It's not easy, it's not easy, and I couldn't do it if I just didn't passionately believe it was the right thing to do. I have so many opportunities from this country . . ." Her voice cracked. "I just don't want to see us fall backwards. You know, this is very personal for me . . ."

In the bus afterward, she ranted at one of her aides, "We never should have gone to Iowa. I knew it. I knew we never should have gone." Now she fretted that she had doomed herself with a "Muskie moment," referring to the late Ed Muskie, the once front-running senator from Maine who had doomed his 1972 presidential campaign by welling up at a campaign event in New Hampshire. Penn had warned her not to show vulnerability. "I've been so wound up in doing the commander-in-chief thing," she said. Later that afternoon she stopped in at her Manchester campaign headquarters, where staffers were buzzing about how she had become choked up at a coffee shop. It played well, they assured her. Hillary thanked them. "Don't expect that too often," she said dryly.

Obama's strategist David Axelrod was on the campaign bus when word came that Clinton had teared up, experienced some sort of breakdown. Some of Obama's aides began chortling about an Ed Muskie moment, but when Axelrod went online and saw a video feed of the incident, he had an uneasy feeling. "Everybody said, 'Oh, Ed Muskie and all that,'" Axelrod later recalled. "But it didn't come across that way to me at all. It came across as a moment of humanity from someone who badly needed to show one."

Obama was making a triumphal march across the state. The press (once so sure of Clinton's "inevitability") sensed History in the Making, the first black presidential nominee.

Several journalists brought their families to Obama campaign rallies to bear witness. But on Jan. 5, at the last debate, Hillary was asked why voters felt that Obama was a more likable figure. "Well, that hurts my feelings," she responded. "But I'll try to go on. He's very likable. I agree with that. I don't think I'm that bad." Obama, barely looking up while he took a note, remarked, "You're likable enough, Hillary."

On Election Day, undecided women voters broke almost entirely Clinton's way. That night, in the press-filing center, *New Yorker* writer Ryan Lizza was putting the finishing touches on a 10,000-word story on Rocket Ship Obama. "I think I'm f——ed," he said. "I have to write a *completely* different story."

Obama was sitting in a coach's office in a high-school gym when the results came in. Axelrod knocked on the door, and Obama stepped outside into the hallway. "It doesn't look like it's going to happen," said Axelrod. Obama closed his eyes and leaned against the wall. He inhaled, exhaled. "This is going to take a while, isn't it?" he asked.

"I think so," Axelrod answered.

John and Cindy McCain greet supporters at the Crowne Plaza Hotel in Nashua, New Hampshire, after the news of his New Hampshire Primary victory. (Photo by Christopher Anderson/Magnum for *Newsweek*)

TWO

Back from the Dead

*By late spring of 2007, John McCain's campaign
was adrift, if not sinking. Then the candidate
found a new narrative: the comeback.*

LIKE A LOT OF AMERICANS, Barack Obama says
his favorite movie is *The Godfather*. John McCain
says his all-time favorite is *Viva Zapata!*, a little-
remembered, highly romanticized 1952 Marlon Brando
biopic. The hero of the movie is Emiliano Zapata, the leader
of a (briefly) successful peasant revolt in Mexico in the early
1900s. McCain loves the idea of a budget-class, guerrilla-
style war against the corrupt establishment. He never got
over being nostalgic about his 2000 insurgency against
George W. Bush and the Republican Party leaders who had
settled on George H.W. Bush's eldest son as heir apparent.
Though himself the scion of a kind of warrior royalty—
his father and grandfather had been admirals, and his
mother came from a wealthy family—McCain was leery of
the overprivileged (and hated being called a "scion"). He

would eventually come to embrace the younger Bush at the 2000 Republican convention, awkwardly hugging a rather startled-looking Bush around the midsection, as high as McCain's war-damaged arms could go. Privately, he told one of his closest aides that he strongly disliked Bush (the word the aide used was "detests").

At the time of the 2000 campaign, McCain had pictured himself as Luke Skywalker, going up against the Death Star. Rumbling along with his aides and a gaggle of mostly friendly reporters in a bus called the Straight Talk Express, he had relished the team spirit—the unit cohesion, in the language of his military past—and the teasing back-and-forth. Not long after the 2000 election, he had spoken of the heady time with a *Newsweek* reporter over a standard-issue McCain breakfast (glazed doughnuts, coffee) in his Senate office. He was sitting at one end of his couch, the purplish melanoma scar down the left side of his face veiled in shadow. "Yeah, we were a band of brothers," he said, his voice low, his eyes shining.

The 2000 race had been a glorious adventure, a heroic Lost Cause. But the fact was that McCain had *lost*. In politics, insurgencies produce memories, not victories. Or so believed John Weaver, McCain's longtime close aide and the man who had first persuaded McCain to start thinking about a presidential run back in 1997. In numerous conversations throughout 2005 and 2006, Weaver, along with other McCain friends and advisers, gently underscored this reality. In their view, Republican nominating politics usually adhered to a rule, attributed variously to Napoleon and Frederick the Great, among others, that God favors big battalions. The key to securing the GOP nomination was to lock up the big money early, round up the best organizers, secure the shiniest endorsements and win the label "inevitable." That's how George W. Bush had beaten McCain and everyone else in 2000, and that's what John McCain needed to do for 2008.

McCain went along, grudgingly. He signed off in the fall of 2006 as his campaign rented sleek, corporate-looking offices in the Crystal City section of Arlington, Va., just across the Potomac River from Washington, D.C. The crystal palace quickly filled with veterans of the Bush-Cheney 2004 campaign, many of whom had never before met McCain. For campaign boss, McCain shoved aside Rick Davis, his campaign manager from 2000, and appointed Terry Nelson, the political director for Bush-Cheney 2004. Boyish and soft-spoken, Nelson was an organization man. His approach was essentially Shock and Awe. By his own admission, he was not the sort of man you would hire for an insurgent-model candidacy of the kind McCain had run in 2000; his relevant experience was more appropriate to crushing that kind of campaign.

McCain was never comfortable playing the front runner. His comment when he first walked through headquarters was "It's awfully big." McCain was ill suited to be the establishment's man. He was suspect to the true believers on the right, the Rush Limbaugh "dittoheads" who regarded him as a RINO (Republican in Name Only). While the Republican right wanted to build a wall and keep out all the immigrants, McCain was trying to forge a compromise—with Ted

Kennedy, no less. The party stalwarts had reason to be doubtful about McCain, who could be salty in his private denunciations. To a couple of his closest advisers he grumbled, "What the f—— would I want to lead *this* party for?"

The McCain campaign was supposed to be a lavish money machine; the draft budget was for more than $110 million. But the money did not come in. Most campaigns can expect 80 to 85 percent of donors to honor their pledges. In the McCain campaign, fewer than half did. "They come, they eat our food, they drink our liquor, they get their pictures taken," said McCain's aide Mark Salter. "But they don't send a check." Most candidates don't like doing the "ask," begging strangers for dollars. McCain virtually stopped making calls, and his chief money raiser, Carla Eudy, stopped asking him to do it. The campaign had boasted that it could raise $50 million in the all-important first quarter of 2007, an amount that might have intimidated the opposition. Instead McCain raised $13 million, less than either Mitt Romney or Rudy Giuliani.

Rick Davis, manager of the 2000 campaign, had not been exiled altogether; he had just been pushed aside, told to talk up the donors and handle what was called "the Mrs. McCain stuff"—seeing to it that Cindy McCain got whatever she needed. In the winter and spring of 2007, what Mrs. McCain got from Davis was an earful about how badly the campaign was going.

CINDY McCAIN HAD NEVER LOVED politics. She understood that she had to be a "Navy wife" and put up with her husband's frequent long absences, but that didn't mean she liked to play the stoic. The daughter of a wealthy Arizona beer distributor, Cindy had been pampered by her father and sent to school at the University of Southern California (USC, which, John liked to tease, really stands for University of Spoiled Children). On the campaign trail, her platinum blond hair pulled back in a sleek but severe style, she was a notably unsmiling presence. During the 2000 campaign, she had been reduced to tears when Republican dirty tricksters started putting out the word that she had been addicted to painkillers (true, but successfully kicked) and that McCain had fathered a love child with a black hooker (the smear artists used photos of the McCains' daughter Bridget, adopted from a Bangladeshi orphanage by Cindy). Cindy had blamed the Bush operation, and she bridled against "those Bush people" now surrounding her husband. Davis did not discourage her complaints.

The crystal palace, in the winter of 2007, turned into a snake pit. The Weaver-Nelson camp blamed Davis's people in fundraising for not drumming up enough money; the Davis camp blamed the Nelson-Weaver management for spending money they didn't have. Davis whispered to Cindy that headquarters was filled with résumé padders and mercenaries who weren't really there out of loyalty to John McCain. The candidate seemed irritated and slightly bewildered. Hearing that the communications shop had just attacked Mitt Romney again, he would ask in genuine bafflement, "Well, why did we do *that*?"

McCain was an inveterate cell-phoner. He was constantly on the phone pressing his staff and his advisers—present and

former—for information. "What's going on?" he would begin the conversation. "What's happening?" As the discussion
seemed to finally wind down, he would push, "What *else*?"
McCain had no use for chains of command, and he used his
cell phone to set up back channels into the campaign hierar-
chy. His calls to dissidents against the campaign leadership
stirred up so much confusion and anxiety that his friend the
former senator Phil Gramm finally advised him to stop.

The candidate looked unhappy and his performances were
lackluster; the money was not rolling in; no one was talking
about the "inevitability" of John McCain. By the late spring
of 2007, McCain's campaign was at best adrift, if not sinking. The problem was not Nelson and Weaver or Davis, the
new Bushians or the old McCainiacs. The problem was
McCain.

To the many reporters who had ridden McCain's bus in
2000, the Straight Talk Express, the candidate was a charming, winning man. He liked to tease and joke, and he could
talk for hours—on the record—about almost any subject. Reporters who spent time with him sensed that beneath the
bluffness there was a sense of grace—that McCain, tortured
in prison, possessed an unusual depth of character, that he
was capable of profound forgiveness of sin, his own and
others. He occasionally held grudges, but usually he dropped
them. He could admit to his faults and often did. He was dis-
arming: "He wore his flaws like a badge of honor and jeal-
ously guards his demons," recalled Carl Cameron, a *Fox News*
reporter who had traveled many miles with him. To say that
McCain was not like most politicians was an almost laugh-

able understatement. Who else was so open and accessible? McCain, for his part, loved reporters: at the 2004 Republican convention, he had invited 50 A-list journos to a fancy French restaurant in New York and toasted them, only half kidding, as "my base."

But McCain's closest friends knew a more complicated man, more human, not necessarily less heroic, but whose virtues were also his flaws. They observed his restlessness and noted that he seemed incapable of serenity, that he could never really relax (except, perhaps, to watch a football game). One Arizona friend observed that he always seemed to be in a rush, as if he were making up for the years he'd lost in prison. McCain seemed to have an almost pathological desire not to be left alone, a hangover, some aides surmised, from his many months in solitary confinement as a POW. He seemed to need to be on the bus sparring with reporters; he was bored by staff briefings on the minutiae of polling and tactics. At one point, when the campaign was talking to charter companies about airplanes, someone suggested a plane for the candidate and staff and a separate plane for the press. The response from several other staffers was, are you kidding? McCain would dump the staff and take the reporters on his plane.

Even his top aides, who tended to be close personal friends as well, sometimes had uneasy feelings about the candidate. Because McCain seemed to live in the moment, because he had no regrets and could move on without looking back, one of his most intimate advisers confessed that he feared he might be dropped at any second, cast off, without warning or much second thought. McCain was loyal, he loved to talk about the band of brothers . . . and yet he could be secretive and evasive. He could be blunt, sometimes scorchingly so . . . but did anyone know what he was really thinking?

For all his gregariousness, McCain was at heart a loner. He was a pilot, a solo fighter jock, not an admiral of the fleet; in the Navy he had relatively little command experience, aside from running an air wing of replacement pilots after he returned from Vietnam. A military brat who moved around with his family, McCain had never been in any one place for long. Called a carpetbagger when he first ran for Congress from Arizona in 1982, he snapped back sarcastically that he would have appreciated the luxury of "growing up and living and spending my entire life in a nice place like the First District of Arizona, but I was doing other things. As a matter of fact, when I think about it now, the place I lived the longest in my life was in Hanoi." But with his aides, he rarely talked about those five and a half years in prison in the Hanoi Hilton.

In the U.S. Senate, McCain had a well-deserved reputation as a straight talker (also as "Senator Hothead"). He did not seem hesitant to get in the face of some lawmaker who, in his view, was feeding at the public trough. He would turn cold and angry, spout profanities and later apologize (it was said that half the Senate had received a note of apology from McCain, an exaggeration, but not by much). At the same time, however, McCain disliked confronting his own friends. He hated to fire anyone from his staff. Not unlike Hillary Clinton, he resisted stepping in to make personnel changes, even when they were overdue.

The closer they got, McCain's friends and advisers found, the more they realized how difficult it was to know or understand this man who could blow hot and cold, who could be comradely yet elusive. One of the psychiatrists who had interviewed McCain after he was freed from North Vietnam in 1973 noted a "slight passive-aggressive trait." That wasn't a character trait he had picked up in prison. As a high-school student (nicknames: "Punk" and "McNasty") and as a young midshipman at the Naval Academy, McCain had been a subversive. He at once revered the Navy—had accepted that he was destined to follow his father and grandfather into the Sea Service—and yet rebelled against it. He seemed to know where the line was, avoiding trouble that would get him kicked out of Annapolis, but racking up enough demerits to graduate fifth from the bottom of his class. McCain showed some of the same passive-aggressiveness toward his own staffers. He would not want to fire them outright, but he would make life uncomfortable for them until they quit. But then, missing them, he never really let go. After Carla Eudy, his chief fundraiser, was pushed out in the spring of 2007, she estimated that she talked more often to the candidate than she had when she was working for him. She thought of the Eagles song "Hotel California," about a hotel where you could check out but never leave. Others compared service to McCain to the CIA: once you were in, you were in forever.

Presidential candidates are not supposed to micromanage their campaigns, but as the amount of money going out of the campaign continued to exceed the amount coming in, McCain could not resist. In May, he sternly ordered his top aides to "slash, slash the budget, right now. Start laying off people." But he could not bring himself to make any changes in the campaign command. McCain was extremely close to John Weaver, who had first pushed him to run and for the next decade traveled all over the country with him testing the waters and building support. (Among Weaver's jobs was combing McCain's hair; McCain's arms cannot reach that high.) A dour-looking man, Weaver was called "Sunny" by the wisecracking candidate. Love is not too strong a word to describe what Weaver felt for McCain. But by the spring of 2007, the two men were quarreling incessantly. "Every day was a struggle with John," Weaver later recalled. "Every phone call was an argument, an awful argument, and I talked to him 18, 19, 20 times a day. He was mad about every little thing, because he had been ginned up to be mad about every little thing—a lot of things that weren't true." The chief "ginner," Weaver suspected, was Davis, stirring up Cindy McCain and the candidate himself.

By SUMMER, McCAIN HAD LESS cash on hand than Ron Paul, the libertarian cult candidate. At a broiling-hot campaign retreat at McCain's family compound in Sedona, Ariz., the candidate stood glumly at his grill, handing out smoky chunks of meat, not saying much. For the weekend after July 4, McCain and his best Senate pal, Lindsey Graham, went to Iraq together. McCain had been under pressure from various party elders and some of his own aides to back off his steadfast support of the war in Iraq. But he was moved by the stoicism of the troops he met there, and also stirred by a pep talk he got from Graham, a smooth talker and true believer in the McCain mystique. Somewhere on the 14-hour plane ride back, McCain said to Graham, "You know we got to keep going; we can't let those guys down." Graham replied, "That's right, John. If they can do it, we can do it."

When McCain returned, he summoned Terry Nelson and Weaver and engaged in a prolonged shouting match over the sorry state of the campaign. Weaver blamed McCain: "Terry didn't set up the system, *you* set up that system, and we believed our own bulls——, and that's how we got in this situation." Weaver stormed out; Nelson quit before he could be fired.

Waiting in the wings was Rick Davis to reprise his 2000 role as campaign manager. Davis put an end to profligacy. The offices and cubicles in the crystal palace began to empty as the staff shrank by more than half. Davis assembled the remnants to work at long tables in a large open space. To one staffer, the place looked a little like a bingo parlor.

The national press had largely stopped paying attention to McCain as his campaign spluttered in the spring and early summer. But on a trip to New Hampshire in mid-July, Mark Salter, McCain's closest adviser and all-purpose amanuensis (he co-authored McCain's bestselling books and wrote his speeches), noticed that the press corps had suddenly swollen, and not just with beat reporters. A number of Washington "Big Feet"—bureau chiefs and pundits and chief political correspondents—had made the trip. They were there to write

McCain's political obituary, Salter realized. He confronted *The Washington Post*'s senior political correspondent, Dan Balz: "You're vultures on a wire here to see when he is gonna clutch his chest and drop dead."

McCAIN KEPT STOICALLY SLOGGING along, but the grim set of his jaw and his dogged left-foot, right-foot determination were plain to see. He dropped his resistance to making fundraising calls, but the donors were still holding back, and the crowds on the trail were small and listless. It was a blue period for McCain; he was sustained mostly by grit.

But then, grit is not something McCain has in short supply. In late summer, an occasional consultant named Steve Schmidt gave him some valuable advice. Schmidt was another veteran of Bush-Cheney '04—he had run the war room, the rapid-response unit. He was a strong believer in developing a simple message and hammering it home.

In a phone call in August, Schmidt asked McCain, "What do you really think is happening in Iraq?" McCain answered, "I think things are getting better. I think the surge is working." Bending to the political winds, McCain had lately become a little equivocal about Iraq in his public comments, but privately he continued to believe that surrendering in Iraq would send a signal of weakness to Al Qaeda and the rest of the world, and that defeat would break the spirit of the U.S. military.

Schmidt understood that this was the character the public needed to see—defiant, passionate, willing to sacrifice his political career for his convictions. This was the candidate who could win in New Hampshire, a state that liked mavericks and did not want to be told whom to vote for by *The Washington Post.*

"Sir," said Schmidt, who treated McCain with military respect (though he had not served himself), "we need to stop hedging on Iraq. You believe in this. You don't think things are getting better; you believe we are winning the war, sir. We need to tell the voters that." He told McCain he needed to get a bunch of his old POW buddies together and travel across the country in the campaign bus McCain had loved so much. Start in San Diego (a Navy town) and end in New Hampshire. Stay in crappy hotels, Schmidt said. Get out some lawn chairs and sit outside and drink a couple of beers with the buddies at night. After all, there was nothing left to lose. "You're a fan of literature. You're a fan of the movies. Plays have three acts. Movies have narrative arcs. Your campaign is dead," said Schmidt. "There is only one narrative left—the comeback. You have no choice, sir."

Schmidt touched McCain's mad-as-hell, romantic streak at just the right moment. In September, McCain embarked on the "No Surrender Tour." (Most of his advisers—the same ones who had wanted him to back off on Iraq—were unenthusiastic; his New Hampshire staff warned, as one of them put it, "Don't bring that bus up here.") McCain's sometime traveling buddy was Senator Graham, who shared his streak of black humor. An avid newspaper reader, McCain took a kind of grim pleasure reading his political obituaries. "We've got 'em right where we want 'em!" he would chortle to seatmate Graham. At some stops, the crowd was composed mostly of aging veterans. "Here's the good news," Graham told McCain after one such event. "The 90-plus crowd is with us. The World War II vets are ready to go back in!"

The campaign continued its rickety path through the fall. At one point, Mark McKinnon, a media adviser who had worked for Bush-Cheney '04, described the difference between the Bush campaigns he had worked on and the McCain campaign as the difference between the Royal British Navy and Capt. Jack Sparrow's ship in *Pirates of the Caribbean*. McCain loved the comparison. He began making guttural pirate noises, punctuating his jokes and one-liners with "Aaarrgh" and occasionally greeting reporters with this oddly cheerful growl. PIRATES FOR MCCAIN T shirts (complete with skull and crossbones) eventually sprouted on the backs of campaign volunteers and even a few reporters. The Straight Talk Express revived; network producers began napping on the bus and watching TV in McCain's seating area when the candidate was busy.

Along about Thanksgiving, reporters began to notice a change. The size of the crowds was increasing, and McCain began to creep up in the polls, especially in New Hampshire. He was blessed by the quality of his opponents. In the grim days of summer, when a *Newsweek* reporter had asked why he shouldn't join the rest of the press corps in reading the last rites for McCain's presidential aspirations, Rick Davis had responded with an incongruously cheerful smile. Nothing personal, he said; our opponents are all good men, some of them are my friends—but politically speaking? "Look, at the end of the day," he said, "the rest of these guys suck." However crude, his judgment was not off base. Ex-businessman Mitt Romney seemed to treat the campaign as a management-consulting project, as if he were selling a product and trying to increase market share. He had no fingertips as a politician and came off as a phony, even when he was perfectly sincere. Rudy Giuliani seemed to be building a cult of Rudy, constantly talking about his performance on 9/11 to a nation that wanted to forget about the terrorist attacks, and he badly miscalculated by believing that he could wait until the Florida primary in late January to make his move. Former senator Fred Thompson seemed old and half asleep. Former governor Mike Huckabee of Arkansas was emerging as an engaging showman and a lively dark horse—but as an evangelical minister with no foreign-policy experience, he almost certainly could not win.

Like a lot of fighter pilots and old sea dogs, McCain was notoriously superstitious. For some mysterious reason, he insisted on sitting in the fourth row of his JetBlue charter plane, as a hapless advance staffer found out when the candidate told her to change seats. In New Hampshire, McCain told his staff to book the same room in the same hotel he'd stayed in during his stunning upset victory over George W. Bush in 2000. He also wore the same lucky green sweater from that night and carried a lucky penny and an Indian feather. On Jan. 8, the day of the New Hampshire primary, McCain was uptight and testy. There was no more joking around. He sharply hushed a couple of well-meaning friends who told him, "Hey, you're going to win."

He won easily. "Mac is back!" went up the raucous chant. Later that night, after his speech, McCain adviser Steve Duprey filled his pockets with the confetti that had showered over the victory crowd. Knowing McCain's superstitious nature, Duprey wanted to make sure he had some lucky confetti on hand at every remaining primary day.

McCain lost Michigan to Romney on Jan. 15, largely because Romney pandered to his boyhood home state by promising to bring back jobs long gone. In South Carolina on Jan. 19, McCain was on edge and his wife, Cindy, even more so. This was the place where the dirty tricksters had slimed the McCains in 2000, and Cindy could not shake off a sense of dread. The weather in Charleston was awful—sleeting rain— and McCain seemed caged, cooped up with his friend Lindsey Graham, who was annoying him by trying to "visualize" victory. By 7 P.M., Cindy and Graham were ready to "jump out the window," Graham later recalled. McCain's 95-year-old mother, Roberta, tried to lighten the mood by cracking jokes about how she wanted to marry Lindsey. The phone rang. It was Liz Sidoti of the Associated Press, telling Schmidt that the AP was about to call the race for McCain. Excited relief spread through the room; some aides began to cry and hug each other. All eyes turned to the TV set, waiting for the cable networks to bring the news. Two minutes passed, then five, then 10 minutes. The phone rang again. It was Sidoti saying the AP had decided to hold back. The projections from its computer model weren't satisfying the analysts—it looked as if Huckabee was closing the gap. "See, Lindsey? This is because of you," McCain said, only half joking.

The excruciating vigil resumed. "We're up, boy, we're up," Graham murmured softly when the numbers turned. "Boy, we're down," McCain replied moments later. (McCain and Graham often call each other "boy," another obscure McCain bonding ritual.) The agony finally ended at 9:20 P.M., when Sidoti called back to say the AP was about to officially declare McCain the winner.

Mark Salter would recall that he had never seen McCain so happy as that night. The 71-year-old torture victim bounded onstage, a little creakily, and Cindy was glowing and regal in a purple suit and pearls. Grinning mischievously, McCain couldn't resist a reference to the 2000 debacle in South Carolina. "What's eight years among friends?" he chortled to the crowd. When his mother drew a roar, McCain walked over and kissed her on the cheek. "Thank you, Momma," he said. He exited the stage as Abba's "Take a Chance on Me" played. He stayed up late into the night, talking with his buddy Graham about how far they had come and what lay ahead. Only bad luck could deny him now.

By late February, Salter had finally stopped waking up each morning with thoughts of a potentially ruinous story racing in his mind. In December, he had felt sure it was coming. *The New York Times* was calling around, asking about McCain's relationship to an attractive lobbyist named Vicki Iseman. In 1999, she had often been seen around McCain's office at the Senate commerce committee, where he was chairman. Friends were calling Salter and asking about the rumors. Was the *Times* about to run an exposé of an extramarital affair between McCain and a lobbyist, for whom he was alleged to have performed legislative favors? Salter had spent hours (including Christmas Day) locating records in an effort to prove that the story was not true. But the rumor mill was grinding on the campaign trail. When a *New York Times* reporter, talking to Romney's press secretary, knocked down gossip that the story would be on page one the next day, Romney joined the conversation and asked, "It's not running?" It was pretty clear that Romney hoped the story would run sometime before the New Hampshire primary.

But weeks passed, and the article did not materialize. Salter heard that the *Times*'s editor, Bill Keller, had spiked the story twice. Salter began to believe the article would not run. Salter could be standoffish, and he was often ironic and sometimes angry. But he was also a romantic, one reason why he was such an effective alter ego for McCain. Salter wanted to believe that the *Times* editors were "grown-ups," as he put it to Schmidt. The accusations were too flimsy and the *Times* was too reputable. "I know them," he told Schmidt. "They're adults. They're not going to hurt a Christian family with no reason."

SCHMIDT WAS NOT SO SURE. He regarded himself as a realist about the media: he was willing to use reporters and even be used by them. He regarded the media as a problem needing vigilant attention. Even the friendliest reporters, the ones whose company he enjoyed at hotel bars, could be expected to turn on the campaign. *The New York Times*, he believed, harbored a clear liberal bias. "Look," he told Salter, "if McCain is the nominee, he's going to have two opponents: whomever the Democrats nominate and *The New York Times*. And *The New York Times* is gonna spend every day trying to help your Democratic opponent beat you, and you've just got to accept that."

On Feb. 21, the *Times* posted a story on its Web site implying that McCain had been romantically involved with Iseman around the time of his bid for the 2000 nomination. The campaign was given two hours' warning. McCain was campaigning in Ohio, and Salter and Schmidt were in Washington. They raced to the airport, where it was snowing and flights were being canceled. Finally boarding a flight to Detroit, where they could rent a car and drive to Toledo, they scrolled their BlackBerrys as the *Times* story popped up online. Schmidt began to gently pound his fist on the seat in front of him.

"This was a mistake for *The New York Times*. This is not only not gonna hurt us, it's gonna help us," Schmidt said, with just a hint of excitement in his voice. "We're gonna go brief McCain. We're gonna tell him to stand up there stoically. Do a press conference. Take every question. Just don't get pissed off." Salter began to feel a little better. The two men discussed damage control. When they got to Detroit, they were going to start calling reporters, telling them that the story wasn't fit to print, that it had been spiked a couple of times before the *Times* finally ran a very thin version—a clumsy attempt to slip hints of illicit romance into a story that purported to be largely about McCain's ties to lobbyists. This was just another sad chapter in the paper's once proud history, they would say—a tawdry sequel to Jayson Blair, the *Times* reporter who got caught fictionalizing his stories.

It was 11:30 P.M. by the time Salter and Schmidt reached the McCains' hotel suite. Cindy was visibly upset. McCain was stone-faced and seething, but silent. Salter started right in: "Y'know what? The story was a mistake. It's a bulls—— story, and it's gonna be easy to fight." The two aides spelled out their strategy for a press conference. "Don't get mad," Salter urged. "Just be calm." McCain said very little, except "See you at the press conference."

The next day McCain flatly denied any romantic involvement with Iseman and excoriated the *Times*. Schmidt's instincts were right: the story proved to be an embarrassment to the newspaper. The pundits turned on the *Times* for running a story with so little apparent evidence; the *Times*'s ombudsman was also critical of the paper. There were a few awkward loose ends. The story claimed that McCain's advisers had warned him to stop seeing Iseman. McCain flatly denied this to reporters. But John Weaver—McCain's old best buddy, now in semi-exile though still talking occasionally to Salter—told the *Times* (and *Newsweek*'s Michael Isikoff) that he had met with Iseman at a restaurant at Union Station and told her to stay away from the senator. Speaking not for attribution, two advisers told *Newsweek* that McCain had indeed been warned to stop seeing Iseman back in December 1999, when he was gearing up for a presidential run. But these details were largely overlooked by the mainstream press, which quickly lost interest in the story.

Schmidt's handling of the Iseman story was a telling moment in the campaign. McCain might like to pal around with reporters, but the lesson was clear: in the end, the liberal press would always turn on you. Salter did not give up on reporters right away, but he came to believe that "gotcha" journalism was pushing aside honest give-and-take. The Straight Talk Express had been fun, but it was not the way to win.

Obama backstage at a rally in New Jersey with Caroline Kennedy and Senator Ted Kennedy during the last full day of campaigning before Super Tuesday. (Photo by Charles Ommanney / *Newsweek*)

THREE

The Long Siege

*The fight between Hillary Clinton and
Barack Obama turned into a grinding stasis that
played out until the very last primary day.*

IN THE DAYS AFTER HIS WIFE'S back-from-the-brink
victory in New Hampshire, Bill Clinton was full of
righteous indignation. The former president had
amassed an 81-page list of all the unfair and nasty things the
Obama campaign had said, or was alleged to have said,
about Hillary Clinton. The press was still in love with
Obama, or so it seemed to Clinton, who complained to
pretty much anyone who would listen. If the press wouldn't
go after Obama, then Hillary's campaign would have to do
the job, the ex-president urged. On Sunday, Jan. 13, Clinton
got worked up in a phone conversation with Donna Brazile,
a direct, strong-willed African-American woman who had
been Al Gore's campaign manager and advised the Clintons
from time to time. "If Barack Obama is nominated, it will be
the worst denigration of public service," he told her, ranting

on for much of an hour. Brazile kept asking him, "Why are you so angry?"

The former president was restless and petulant; that was obvious. Exactly why was a psychologist's guessing game. He seemed anxious that his wife was blowing the chance to get the Clintons back in the White House. At some deeper level, the armchair shrinks speculated, he was jealous of her. Or, in some strange way, he may have been envious of Obama. Clinton was proud of the fact that some blacks called him "America's first black president," because of his comfort and empathy with African-Americans. Obama was upstaging him by threatening to truly become America's first black president. More vexingly, Obama, in remarks to some reporters in Nevada, had praised Ronald Reagan as a true change agent and seemingly dismissed Bill Clinton as an incidental politician. It was always hard for Clinton to be anything but the most amazing person in the room, the "smartest boy in the class," as author David Maraniss had once described him. Clinton wanted to be a major player in his wife's campaign, and he used an office sometimes inhabited by Mark Penn or Mandy Grunwald at Clinton headquarters in Arlington, Va., just outside Washington. But the staff, including the campaign manager, Patti Solis Doyle, found his presence, complete with Secret Service, to be uncomfortable, sometimes intimidating. They were happier when he was on the road—that is, as long as he stayed on message, which was never for very long.

Bill Clinton was enormously effective at the Nevada caucuses on Jan. 19, working the casinos in his larger-than-life way, charming the off-duty waitresses and croupiers. Hillary's narrow victory in Nevada had sustained her post-New Hampshire comeback momentum. The former president wanted to go to South Carolina for the next Democratic test, the Jan. 26 primary. He was sure his touch with African-American voters would blunt Obama's natural advantage (almost half the Democratic voters in South Carolina are black). The campaign staff was not so sure, and scheduled him for only the briefest of visits. But Hillary sided with her husband when the staff briefed her on their minimalist approach to South Carolina. "This is crazy," she said. "Bill needs to go to South Carolina."

He was a disaster. He turned purple yelling at reporters for asking annoying questions. He pointedly compared Obama to Jesse Jackson, who had won the South Carolina caucuses in 1984 and 1988 by appealing directly to black votes. The liberal establishment was appalled—the president seemed to be clumsily playing the race card by trying to marginalize Obama as the "black candidate." Blacks were also put off. Hillary Clinton lost the African-American vote in South Carolina by 86 to 14. At Clinton headquarters, a meeting was hastily convened and a simple message went out: you cannot dis Obama in any way that suggests race. A campaign emissary secretly approached Jesse Jackson. Would he write a letter saying, in effect, no big deal? Jackson replied that he wasn't offended by Clinton's remarks—but declined to say so in a public letter. The Clintons could see their black base, so carefully and genuinely built up over the years, beginning to crumble. The old civil-rights generation was in an awkward place. New York Rep. Gregory Meeks, a member of the Congressional Black Caucus, told Harold Ickes, "You don't understand what it's like. We get called 'house Negro' and 'handkerchief head' by our constituents because we're supporting Hillary." Rep. John Lewis, a hero of the movement (he had been beaten repeatedly while demonstrating in the South in the '60s) and a conscience of the Democratic Party, switched his support from Clinton to Obama.

SEN. EDWARD KENNEDY HAD a difficult phone conversation with Bill Clinton about his divisive campaigning. "Well, they started it," Clinton told Kennedy. "I don't think that's true," said Kennedy. On Jan. 28, Senator Kennedy and, perhaps more significant, Caroline Kennedy, daughter of John F. Kennedy, held a press conference in Washington to endorse Obama. Clinton campaign aides were distraught and partly blamed Hillary. Despite urging from the staff, she had failed to call Caroline to enlist her support. For all her brassiness and grit onstage, Hillary was privately reluctant to call donors and supporters. She didn't really like arm-twisting one-on-one. She was no LBJ, thought Harold Ickes.

Caroline Kennedy had never endorsed a candidate who was not a member of the Kennedy clan. But she wrote a *New York Times* op-ed casting Obama in the mold of John F. Kennedy. Solis Doyle saw the op-ed and thought, "Oh, my God, we're done."

For the record, the Obama campaign did not worry that race would swing the election. "I think we may lose some votes, but we also may gain some votes because of it," said David Axelrod. "I don't think it will determine the out-

come." But when asked about race, Obama campaign officials often seemed touchy and guarded, as if race was a subject best not discussed. In fact, they had reason to worry that
racial prejudice could become a factor, albeit in subtle ways
and blended with other biases. A good part of Obama's appeal was that he was post-racial (although Obama himself
shied away from this somewhat utopian notion). For some
voters, however, race mattered.

Polling on race is notoriously difficult; voters rarely admit
to prejudice. Polls suggested that somewhere between 10 and
30 percent of voters thought that race would be an important
factor in the election. Some of these were black voters who
were likely to vote for Obama, and some were white. Few
whites were flat-out racists, and most of those would vote Republican anyway. But some older and working-class voters,
particularly in Appalachia, the mountainous spine that runs
from upper New York State to the Deep South, harbored
lingering apprehensions and resentments toward African-
Americans. Their motives were often mixed and hard to read.
In critical swing states like Ohio and Pennsylvania, these voters potentially held the balance of power; they had once been
solid New Deal Democrats but had broken away to vote for
Reagan in the 1980s, and now their allegiance was up for
grabs. The Obama staffers did not believe that Clinton (or the
Republicans in the fall) would make a naked appeal on racial
lines. On the other hand, they well understood that clever political operatives could play on fears of Obama as "the Other,"
an exotic blend of dark skin and alien background. They
could point out, in thinly veiled ways, that Obama did not

share their cultural values—they could paint him as a Harvard elitist, a professor type who looked down on gun owners and wanted to turn America into a mongrel nation. Obama's middle name (Hussein) and Muslim ancestry on his father's side were a problem. Polls consistently showed that more than 10 percent of voters thought Obama was Muslim, no matter how often he made clear that he was Christian.

Axelrod thought that Bill Clinton's remark about Jesse Jackson was a gratuitous way of injecting race into the campaign. "Pretty darn intentional," he told a reporter in late January. Axelrod nurtured a healthy paranoia, and he didn't entirely trust the Clintons not to play on the politics of fear. He thought of the Clinton campaign as Jaws, he told the reporter. The water might seem calm now, but . . .

Obama continued to appear to float above it all. In late November, he had met with a group of successful black women in public life that called itself the "Colored Girls Club." The lunch had been arranged by Donna Brazile, who counseled Obama as well as Clinton. Obama told the group that as far as he was concerned, race would not become a topic; he made clear that he would not play identity politics. In South Carolina, the Obama campaign refused to indulge in the time-honored, if slightly disreputable, practice of dispensing "walking-around money" to activists and preachers in the black community. The Clintons, by contrast, continued to hand out the usual favors and cash. Obama not only won the black vote overwhelmingly, he also won the state of South Carolina by 30 points. The press went back to calling him the favorite to win the nomination. As he watched Bill Clinton's favorability rating drop 17 points in a single week around the South Carolina primary, Obama didn't say anything, Axelrod observed. The candidate just shook his head—and smiled.

It may have been a Cheshire-cat grin, but Obama was not a gloater. There was no high-fiving or obvious schadenfreude. As Axelrod saw him, Obama didn't enjoy a good hate. That would be a waste of time and emotion, and Obama was, if nothing else, highly disciplined.

Obama carefully conserved his energy. He was not a man of appetites, like Bill Clinton, who would grab whatever goodie passed by on the tray. Obama was abstemious. Indeed, to the reporters following him, he appeared very nearly anorexic. Most candidates gain the Campaign 10 (or 15). Hillary was struggling with her waistline, as she gamely knocked back shots and beers in working-class bars and gobbled the obligatory sausage sandwiches thrust at her in greasy spoons along the Trail of the White Working-Class Voter. Obama, by contrast, lost weight. He regularly ate the same dinner of salmon, rice and broccoli. At Schoop's Hamburgers, a diner in Portage, Ind., he munched a single french fry and ordered four hamburgers—to go. At the Copper Dome Restaurant, a pancake house in St. Paul, Minn., he ordered pancakes—to go. (An AP reporter wondered: who gets pancakes for the road?) A waiter reeled off a long list of richly topped flapjacks, but Obama went for the plain buttermilk, saying, "I'm kind of traditionalist." Reporters joked that if he ate a single bite of burger or pancake once the doors of his dark-tinted SUV closed, they'd eat their BlackBerrys. Frustrated by reporters fishing for trivial "gaffes," Obama did not like coming back to the plane to talk to the press. As he trudged back from time to time to deal with the reporters' incessant questions, he looked like a suburban dad, slump-shouldered after a long day at the office, taking out the trash.

His one true recreation and release was basketball. In early February, a reporter joined Obama's standard game, whose regulars included some good players, including Michelle Obama's brother, Craig Robinson, a former Princeton player who coaches basketball at Oregon State University, and Reggie Love, Obama's "body man," his all-purpose valet, who stands 6 feet 4 and had played at Duke. Obama was wearing long sweatpants; alone among the players he did not remove them to reveal the skinny legs beneath. Obama is not a natural under the hoop. He doesn't glide. His motion is herky-jerky, from the dangerously high bounce of his dribble to the way he pumps his knees when he runs, chest out, like an Army recruit running in formation. But he could show surprising quickness, snapping a crossover dribble in front of an inattentive defender and driving past him for a layup—a savvy departure from the unhurried, deliberate pace at which he usually plays.

OBAMA HAS ALWAYS BEEN FIERCELY competitive and not above stacking his team with the best players. This led to at least one loud argument on the court with his friend Alexi Giannoulias, the Illinois state treasurer, in the tense days before the Iowa caucuses. Obama had loaded his team with Love and some other hot shots, and Giannoulias's team was losing badly. "So I got mad and started yelling at him—'I want to win too!' " recalled Giannoulias. "And it got under his skin." Obama responded, with rare heat, "I don't care who I play with. I'll play with anybody! You want to switch teams? We can switch teams if you want!" Giannoulias declined, out of pique more than anything, he recalled. "And then he just gave me this smile," Giannoulias said, mimicking Obama's signature smile, teeth flashing, eyes crinkled, chin slightly tucked in, a surprising gleam of warmth, guaranteed to disarm.

Obama's slightly ethereal presence on the campaign trail was balanced by his down-to-earth wife, who had her own travel schedule and was beginning to appear on women's shows like *The View*. The idea was to show her as an appealing mom and regular gal—and also, as the situation required, a classy woman. She was all of that, and yet to some voters she was not a reassuring figure.

Michelle Obama is not ascetic like her husband. She has long been familiar with Chicago's chicest clothing stores, and she'll "eat a cheeseburger in a heartbeat," said Cheryl Rucker-Whitaker, her close friend from Chicago (Rucker-Whitaker's husband, Eric, is a friend of Obama's from Harvard days and often plays basketball with him). Michelle's favorite drink, said Rucker-Whitaker, is champagne. "She likes clothes, she's always loved clothes, she loves purses, she loves getting a manicure, getting her hair done. She really is a girly girl." Tall and beautiful, she caused flutters (and raised a few eyebrows) when she appeared onstage at a victory celebration dressed in a *soignée*, early-'60s style reminiscent of Jacqueline Kennedy. She was a Princeton and Harvard Law grad, formidable and elegant but at the same time playful.

While her husband was a dreamer and serious, she was the practical one and a bit of a jokester and teaser. There was no doubting their physical attraction. Reporters liked to snicker at how much looser the candidate seemed after spending the occasional night at home or on the road with his wife.

She was also more deeply rooted in black America than Obama, whose mother had been white and who had grown up in Hawaii and Indonesia. Though no one on the Obama staff talked about it much, there was no doubt that Michelle's self-conscious blackness was unsettling to that narrow but important slice of swing voters, the so-called Reagan Democrats, older working-class voters in the Rust Belt swing states of Michigan, Ohio and Pennsylvania. Michelle was from the South Side of Chicago; the white political machine of Chicago had intentionally segregated Chicago, cutting off the South Side with a highway, and racial politics were played hard in the place Michelle grew up. At Princeton in the early 1980s, Michelle felt like an outsider at an elitist college that began taking blacks only after World War II. Her senior thesis for the sociology department examined whether African-American graduates of Princeton identified with "white society" as they enjoyed upward mobility. Beneath its academic formalism, her writing has a rueful quality—she clearly (and accurately) expected to be drawn into the white world upon graduation, but wrote that, even so, she expected to "remain on the periphery of society; never becoming a full participant." In fact, she became a lawyer at a fancy Chicago law firm (where she met her future husband, who was interning for the summer from Harvard) and later a high-level hospital administrator. But she never forgot her roots. When some African-Americans began grumbling that her husband was not "black enough," Michelle was the one who directly confronted the issue, bluntly telling a South Side of Chicago crowd, "Stop that nonsense."

For the most part, Michelle Obama was a poised and confident campaigner. But in late February, when her husband was on a roll, winning caucus after caucus, she slipped up. She told a Milwaukee audience, "For the first time in my adult lifetime, I am really proud of my country, because it feels like hope is finally making a comeback." The Republicans quickly jumped on the intimation that she had not been proud of her country before then. The next day, Cindy McCain told a rally, "I'm proud of my country. I don't know about you—if you heard those words earlier—I'm very proud of my country." Right-wing talk radio began to portray Michelle as a latter-day Angela Davis, a fire-breathing '60s-type black radical, but the mainstream press steered clear of any race baiting. So did the Clinton campaign. In March, Mark Penn suggested that the campaign target Obama's "lack of American roots" and drape Hillary in the flag as much as possible. The idea seemed to be to subtly emphasize Obama's "otherness." To the Clintons' credit, they chose not to go down this route, at least not in any overt way.

Sometimes it seemed as though Hillary Clinton's campaign staffers were more interested in destroying each other than Obama. Patti Solis Doyle was finally fired on Feb. 10, and a messy scene greeted her replacement, Maggie Williams.

STAFFERS WERE TRYING TO WORK, sort of, and ignore the sounds coming from the office of communications director Howard Wolfson. "He's going to ruin this f——ing campaign!" shouted Phil Singer, Wolfson's deputy. No one was quite sure who "he" was, but most assumed it was Penn, the chief strategist who was in more or less constant conflict with Hillary's other top advisers. Wolfson said something indistinct in response, and Singer cut loose, "F—— you, Howard," and stormed out of his office. Policy director Neera Tanden had the misfortune of standing in his path. "F—— you, too!" screamed Singer. "F—— you," Tanden started. "And the whole f——ing cabal," Singer, now standing on a chair, shouted loudly enough to be heard by the entire war room. "I'm done." Within a week or two Singer was back, still steaming and swearing. "If the house is on fire, would you rather have a psychotic fireman or no fireman at all?" Wolfson explained to Williams. A former top aide to Bill Clinton, Williams was regarded as a grown-up, but she wasn't eager to play hall monitor. She had been living quietly with her husband on Long Island, away from the Clinton melodrama, and she didn't appear to have her heart in the battle when a reporter later met with her in the spring of 2008. At the time, commentators were beginning to accuse Hillary of running as the White Candidate. An African-American woman, Williams seemed almost despondent worrying about the effect on young staffers, black and white, of being accused of racism.

Even though the campaign raised more than $100 million before Iowa, money was chronically short. "The cupboard is bare," Harold Ickes announced after New Hampshire at a stunned staff meeting. No one seemed quite sure where it had all gone, though there were a lot of bitter jokes about Hillary's penchant for G4 business jets and Mark Penn's hefty bills for polling and direct mail. Fundraising was getting tougher that winter. A top aide told a *Newsweek* reporter, "Our donors were so disillusioned, particularly with Bill Clinton. The whole Clinton *mishegoss*—people said, if she can't control him in the campaign, how could she control him in the White House? We took a pounding." The campaign aides suggested that the Clintons loan $5 million from their personal fortune before the Super Tuesday primaries on Feb. 5. "Let's do it," Bill Clinton said immediately, but Solis Doyle could hear hesitation in Hillary's voice. She came around, and when word got out that she was tapping her own money, contributions poured in—many from women.

Shortly after Williams took over, she called a major meeting for senior staff. Penn was given the floor, and he began to walk through all the iterations of Hillary slogans: "Solutions for America," "Ready for Change, Ready to Lead," "Big Challenges, Real Solutions: Time to Pick a President . . ." Penn marched down the long list.

But then he seemed to get a little lost. "Um, uh, 'Working for Change, Working for You' . . . " There was silence, then sniggers, as Penn tried to remember all the bumper stickers, which, run together, sounded absurd and indistinguishable. "Ehhh . . . 'The Hillary I Know' . . . " Penn trailed off, and the meeting moved on.

But it was Penn who finally came up with an ad that worked, on the eve of the Ohio and Texas primaries in early

March, when the Clinton campaign was in true do-or-die mode. It began with the sound of a phone ringing in the hours before dawn. Accompanied by portentous music, the ad played to the insecurities of the so-called security moms, who had been shaken by 9/11 and had voted heavily for George W. Bush in 2004. Penn called the "Red Phone 3 A.M." ad a "game changer." Mandy Grunwald, the campaign's ad maker, had opposed it. When someone in the room at a senior staff meeting said, "Great ad!" Grunwald, who was talking by speakerphone, snapped, "This is Mark's ad, not my ad."

Morale was at a low ebb in the Clinton campaign by early March. Incredibly, the campaign had been caught by surprise by Obama's tortoise-and-hare strategy. While Hillary won some big states on Super Tuesday, including New York, California, New Jersey and—take that, Ted Kennedy!—Massachusetts, Obama had been racking up delegates in smaller states, particularly caucus states, where he was organized and Clinton was not. Given the way delegates were apportioned, Obama had amassed a nearly insurmountable lead by the time of the Texas and Ohio primaries on March 4. At one meeting around the time of Super Tuesday, Ickes tried—for the umpteenth time, it seemed—to explain the mechanics of proportional representation. When President Clinton said, "Oh, hell, we didn't have this stuff in 1992," Ickes nearly "fell off his chair," as he later put it, because the system had been essentially the same back then. Ickes grumbled to reporters that Penn didn't even know that California wasn't winner-take-all; Penn denied it.

But Hillary did win Ohio and she did win Texas, though narrowly, and once more she had stepped back from the brink. For Obama, there was some disturbing news in the breakdown of the voting results. He had crossed over the demographic divide in industrial Wisconsin in February, winning older and blue-collar voters, white as well as black. But in Ohio the gap stubbornly returned: Hillary was the darling of older, white working-class voters. The Obama camp was beginning to suspect that the Clinton campaign, while assiduously avoiding any race baiting by the candidate or her senior staff or advisers, was perfectly content to let others do the dirty work, operating through surrogates and the bottom-feeding press. A picture of Obama in Somali garb was leaked to the *Drudge Report*. Clinton surrogate Rep. Stephanie Tubbs Jones of Ohio (who was African-American) said that Obama shouldn't be ashamed to be seen in his "native clothes." In Youngstown, Ohio, the president of the International Machinists Union endorsed Clinton; its president, Tom Buffenbarger, took a swipe at Obama at a Hillary rally, shouting, "I've got news for all the latte-drinking, Prius-driving, Birkenstock-wearing trust-fund babies crowding in to hear him speak! He won't stand a chance against the Republican attack machine!" Reporters noticed that in the bathroom there were copies of an infamous "Obama is a Muslim" e-mail printed out and strewn about.

Obama was not one to cast blame, at least not too obviously or too loudly. After his campaign spent $20 million to win Texas and still lost, he ran through a list of mistakes with his staff, not laying any blame on anyone in particular. He stood up to leave, and as he walked out of the conference room of campaign headquarters on Michigan Avenue, he turned around and said, "I'm not yelling at you guys." He took another few steps and turned around again and said, "Of course, after blowing through $20 million in a couple of weeks, I could yell at you. But . . ." He paused. "I'm not yelling at you." He laughed and walked out the door.

Obama had to strain to stay cool when the Reverend Wright fiasco hit in mid-March. Later that spring, after the hubbub had abated and Obama sat down to give his version of events, he was puzzled, chagrined and a little defensive. His advisers saw Jeremiah Wright as a true threat to Obama's candidacy. For Obama, the fiery and vain reverend was a continuing source of vexation and personal pain.

Obama told a *Newsweek* reporter that he had known from the beginning that Wright could be trouble. Shortly before Obama announced for the presidency in February 2007, Wright had made some "pretty incendiary" remarks to *Rolling Stone* magazine, Obama recalled. Still, he had not wanted to sever his ties to Wright. Obama had long regarded the preacher as a kind of "uncle." In his memoirs, he had credited Wright with "bringing me to Jesus"—as well as showing him the power of the black church as a community organizer. Wright had married Obama and baptized his daughters. Obama told the *Newsweek* reporter that, though he had been Wright's parishioner at Trinity United Church of Christ for almost two decades, he was often away campaigning, which meant attending other churches, or doing something else with his young family on Sunday mornings. He had, he said, missed many of Wright's sermons.

But back in early February 2007, as he read Wright's heated rhetoric about racial injustice in America, printed in the *Rolling Stone* story titled "The Radical Roots of Barack Obama," Obama had thought to himself, "This doesn't sound real good." In a few days, Wright was scheduled to give the invocation at Obama's announcement ceremony at the state capitol in Springfield, Ill. Partly because he wanted to protect Wright's church from getting entangled in politics, Obama called Wright and told him, "You know what, you probably shouldn't introduce me. There's going to be about 500 press credentials there; you don't want a whole bunch of mikes suddenly stuck in your face without any preparation or expectation." Wright, as would later become excruciatingly clear, loved microphones, the more the better, but this time he got the message. He would stay off-stage. "I know that disappointed him," Obama recalled, "and I think he might have felt some anger about that."

Wright did not stay quiet for long. He soon gave his version of what happened between him and Obama to a reporter from *The New York Times*. He told the *Times* that one of Obama's advisers had "talked him into disinviting me," and that Obama had told him, "You can get pretty rough in the sermons, so what we've decided is that it's best for you not to be out in public." Obama was miffed when he saw Wright's comments, but decided not to break with him then and there. "He was retiring; I had a strong commitment to the church community. . . . My instinct was to let him stay out of the limelight and not make a bigger deal out of it," Obama recalled to the reporter. However, Obama said that he had told his staff: "Let's pull every single sermon that Wright made, because it could be an issue, and it could be attributed to me, and let's at least know what we're dealing with." He added: "That never got done."

The normally careful Obama team dropped the ball. Axelrod told the *Newsweek* reporter, "I had been asking" for a "readout of all his sermons," but "I didn't get it." (He blamed himself for not following up.) Instead, the campaign watched with growing dismay on the evening of Thursday, March 13, 2008—less than two weeks after the Texas and Ohio primaries—as ABC News aired video clips of the Reverend Wright, delivering a sermon on the Sunday after September 11 declaring that "America's chickens are coming home to roost" for its own acts of "terrorism" and fulminating, "God damn America . . . that's in the Bible! For killing innocent people! God damn America!"

As it happened, Obama was in the middle of another potential mess, dealing with questions about his relationship with Tony Rezko, a Chicago fixer convicted of extorting bribes from lawmakers. In 2006, Obama had bought a small piece of property next to his Chicago home from Rezko— nothing illegal; the Obamas had paid a fair price—but as Obama acknowledged, any personal financial dealing with an influence peddler like Rezko looked bad, especially for a would-be political reformer. That Thursday night in March, as the Reverend Wright story was exploding on cable TV— an endless loop of video clips of Wright ranting—Obama was scheduled to go to the *Chicago Tribune* offices the next day and spend "as long as necessary" answering questions about Rezko. During his nearly three-hour grilling at the *Tribune* building on March 14, Obama patiently answered questions, in a thorough if lawyerly way, until there were no more.

Obama was worn out, or should have been. But that same night, he announced to David Axelrod, "I want to do a speech on race." Axelrod's own instinct was to get as far away from the Reverend Wright as possible. Other top staffers were also wary of making any broad statements about race. Obama's top staffers avoided the topic of race, not only publicly, but in their internal deliberations. Only one of the top staffers, Valerie Jarrett, was black. She would occasionally push the campaign to be more race-conscious, insisting that Obama's ads in Iowa include some photos of blacks as well as whites. But other top staffers saw Obama's racial ambiguity as an asset. If black voters wanted to claim him as the black candidate, fine. If voters wanted to see him as biracial or postracial, that was fine, too. David Plouffe thought that race was mostly a distraction—his eye was always on the numbers, on racking up the delegates. He did not want Obama in any way to be defined by racial politics.

Obama himself had an intuitive sense of when to emphasize his blackness and when not to. When he was speaking to crowds of black voters, he would use a deeper voice and seem more casual and instinctive; with whites, his voice would become flatter and more nasal, his attitude more deliberate. He had a way of telling his black supporters to just shrug off racial innuendo. He used a phrase borrowed from Malcolm X to warn black voters to ignore Internet rumors (like the one that he had taken an oath of office by swearing on a Qur'an). "They're trying to bamboozle you," Obama said at one event in South Carolina in January. "It's the same old okie-doke. Y'all know about okie-doke, right? . . . They try to bamboozle you. Hoodwink ya. Try to hoodwink ya." He seemed to catch himself: "All right, I'm having too much fun here," he said, and changed the topic. Obama knew when to distance himself from black nationalists. Over Valerie Jarrett's objections (she was afraid he would alienate black voters), he had denounced the Rev. Louis Farrakhan during a debate in the fall.

Wright's rants needed to be answered. But how? There was no great internal debate within Obama's staff, in part because no one really knew what to do. But Obama did. Although, back in November, he had breezily told Donna Brazile and her "Colored Girls" group that he would not bring up race, in fact his own search for his racial identity was central to his being, and he knew that sooner or later he might have to broach the subject with voters. For several months, he had been thinking about giving a broader speech on the subject of race, and now the moment had arrived. Obama had his own sense of timing and purpose. He knew that Wright's remarks could stir racial fears that could become a cancer on the campaign unless some steps were taken to cut it out, and that he was the only one skillful enough to attempt the operation.

Obama spent much of the next three nights working on the speech, which he essentially wrote himself. Delivered at an appropriate setting—a museum devoted to the U.S. Constitution in Philadelphia—his half-hour address was a tour de force, the sort of speech that only Barack Obama could give. He had taken some saccharine but sincere advice from his mother—to judge not, to always look for the good in people—and internalized a true sense of tolerance. He had the ability to empathize with both sides—to summon the fear and resentment felt by blacks for years of oppression, but also to talk about how whites (including his grandmother) could fear young black men on the street, and how whites might resent racial preferences for blacks in jobs and schools. He ended with a moving scene, a story of reconciliation between an older black man and a young white woman.

When he walked backstage at the Constitution museum, he found everyone in tears—his wife, his friends and his hardened campaign aides. Only Obama seemed cool and detached. The speech was "solid," he said, as his entourage, tough guys like Axelrod and former deputy attorney general Eric Holder, choked up. The candidate had seemed unflappable the whole weekend, his late nights notwithstanding. He was, from time to time, given to moments of mild amusement. While the Obamas and their aides were dining the night before, Marty Nesbitt, Obama's close friend and basketball buddy, called Obama on his cell phone and said, "Man, look, this is like a blessing in disguise." Obama held the phone away and said to the table, dryly, "Nesbitt says this is a blessing in disguise." On the other end, Nesbitt could hear the laughter. "Really," Nesbitt spluttered, "this is really a blessing in disguise." Obama replied, "Yeah, well . . ." and Nesbitt could hear more raucous laughter.

But it was a blessing in disguise. Wright gave Obama a chance to deal directly with issues that had been the source of whispering or underhanded attacks in the lower precincts of politics, to take the high road on a matter of pressing national importance but on a subject that can be difficult to honestly discuss. He had shown calm good judgment.

Nonetheless, a close reading of the speech suggests more than a hint of personal grandiosity. Obama was giving the voters a choice: they could stay "stuck" in a "racial stalemate." Or they could get beyond it—by, well, voting for him. "We can play Reverend Wright's sermons on every channel, every day, and talk about them from now until the election. . . . We can pounce on some gaffe by a Hillary supporter as evidence that she's playing the race card, or we can speculate on whether white men will flock to John McCain. . . . We can do that. But if we do, I can tell you that in the next election, we'll be talking about some other distraction. And then another one. And then another one. And then nothing will change." But if you vote for me—now—this time, Obama strongly implied, blacks and whites could come together and deal with the greater challenges facing the country, of health care and education, want and war. At times like this, Obama seemed to project that he was "the One" that Oprah had rhapsodized about. In the speech, he was careful to be modest ("I have never been so naive as to believe that we can get beyond our racial divisions in a single election cycle, or with a single candidacy—particularly a candidacy as imperfect as my own"). But the implicit message was: I Am the One, Choose Me—or this historic moment may pass, never to be recovered.

THE CLINTON CAMPAIGN WAS careful not to exploit the Wright imbroglio, or at least careful not to get caught at it. At Clinton headquarters, Harold Ickes took a call from Greg Sargent, a reporter from *Talking Points Memo*, one of the new generation of bloggers shaking up the old media. Sargent wanted to know, does Wright ever come up in conversations with superdelegates? The superdelegates, party leaders and top congressional Democrats, were Clinton's last hope as Obama rolled toward a majority of elected delegates. They could, theoretically at least, save her candidacy, though they would have to buck the popular vote to do so. Ickes talked to superdelegates every day, trying to hang on to their support. He told TPM that, yes, the superdelegates were concerned about Wright. He soon received a call from Maggie Williams, the campaign boss. Harold, she said, we don't need to be talking about the Reverend Wright.

Hillary Clinton believed that Obama's problems with white working-class voters made him unelectable, and she could be blunt about it when she got on the phone with superdelegates who threatened to switch to Obama. "Bill, he can't win!" she shouted on the phone to Gov. Bill Richardson of New Mexico. The Clintons were particularly anxious to cultivate the support of Richardson, who was popular with Hispanics. Bill Clinton had watched the Super Bowl with Richardson; cameras recorded the scene—two slightly overweight middle-aged men catching a ball game but not looking all that comfortable in each other's company. In the end, Richardson endorsed Obama. James Carville, the Clintons' favorite hit man, compared Richardson to Judas.

The Clintons' dream of restoration was dying. Yet, curiously, in many ways Hillary Clinton found her voice in the spring of 2008. At rallies, recalled Geoff Garin, a Democratic pollster who was brought in in a last-ditch attempt to bring peace and order to the campaign, people would come up to the senator and say, "Don't give up." At a debate in Austin, Texas, she gave a very moving closing statement about the people who had it much tougher than she did. Hoarse and bleary-eyed, she bounced around the country (this time in a charter plane with staff and press—no more private business jets), performing with a combination of gumption and grace.

But she undercut her diminishing chances in April by inexplicably boasting that she had come under sniper fire at an airport in the Balkans during her husband's presidency. She was trying to show that she was a battle-hardened global peacemaker, but since there were videotapes of her being greeted by happy schoolchildren on the tarmac, the press had a field day mocking her. Obama made his own gaffe—telling some rich San Francisco fundraisers that the working-class people in Pennsylvania clung to guns and God out of "bitterness." There was some truth to Obama's off-hand remark (the definition of a "gaffe," columnist Michael Kinsley wrote, is a politician telling the truth). But to many proud and faithful gun-owning members of the working class, Obama was just plain wrong and certainly condescending. The "bitterness" remark risked long-term damage. It opened him to the charge that he was an effete academic snob, out of touch with working-class people.

The campaign drifted into a kind of grinding stasis, with Clinton unable to overcome Obama's lead but Obama unable to finally clinch the nomination. The low point for Obama came at the end of April, when the Reverend Wright popped up again. First in a sympathetic interview with Bill Moyers on PBS, then in a thumping speech to the NAACP and finally in an over-the-top performance at the National Press Club, Wright did his best to draw the spotlight back on him and on his wide set of grievances. Egged on by a claque of cheering black ministers at the press club, Wright delivered what Alessandra Stanley of *The New York Times* described as "a rich, stem-winding brew of black history, Scripture, hallelujahs and hermeneutics." Waiting to go live for the event, MSNBC called David Axelrod for comment on Wright. "He is doing his own thing," said Axelrod, wearily. "There's nothing we can do about it."

In Chicago, Eric Whitaker, Obama's close friend, watched the rebroadcast with alarm. "I called him [Obama] that night and told him that he really needed to watch the video of it," Whitaker said. "He told me, 'I don't know if I can. I think it's going to be too painful to watch.'"

A week later, with close contests in Indiana and North Carolina looming, Whitaker and two others of Obama's close friends, Marty Nesbitt and Valerie Jarrett, went to support the candidate as he attended a Stevie Wonder concert and worked a factory late shift in North Carolina. It was a "low period," Jarrett recalled, as the four of them stood in the drizzle and the mud waiting for the factory workers. Obama was "hurt" and "struggling," she recalled. Nesbitt found him anxious and fretful, shaken "off his usual steady state." Obama liked to control his own story, and now he was being "subjected to someone else's craziness," Whitaker recalled. The three friends tried to lighten Obama's mood, joking around about nothing in particular. "We had him laughing for a minute," said Nesbitt. "But it was laughter to keep from crying," said Whitaker. Then Axelrod arrived to announce, "The polls in Indiana look really, really bad," and everyone shouted, "Come *o-o-o-o-on*," recalled Jarrett.

But the next night Obama won big in North Carolina even as he was losing narrowly in Indiana. On NBC, Tim Russert, regarded as an oracle by his peers and most of the political world, pronounced, "We now know who the Democratic nominee is going to be, and no one is going to dispute it." It was finally over—except that it wasn't, quite—not until Hillary Clinton surrendered.

She was determined to campaign to the last, hoping against hope that the superdelegates would come around to her argument that Obama was unelectable. This was not an argument that he wanted to get caught up in. From the headquarters of the "No-Drama Obama" campaign the word went out: do not engage, do not inflame, do not say or do anything that might suggest Clinton did not have the right to finish the campaign. On one conference call, someone said, "We've just got to keep biting our lips, biting our lips." Adman Jim Margolis piped up, "OK, but my lip is starting to hurt."

Obama shook off his disappointment about Wright and kept on campaigning, though it was obvious that he was not happy burning time and money that could have been spent turning to John McCain. On May 20, the night of the primaries in Oregon (a satisfying win in a liberal state) and Kentucky (another discouraging blowout in Appalachia; he had lost West Virginia the week before by 41 points), he stood off-stage at the Des Moines Historical Society Museum in Iowa. He had wanted to go back to the state of his first great triumph to give a speech unofficially kicking off the fall campaign, even though Clinton officially was still in the race. "That's an interesting belt buckle," he said to Michelle, mischievously. She feigned offense and said, "I am interesting, next to you. Surprise, surprise, a blue suit, a white shirt and a tie." Obama grinned and bent down until he was almost at eye level with her waist. He jabbed a playful finger toward her belt buckle, and let loose his inner nerd. "The lithium crystals! Beam me up, Scotty!" Obama squeaked, laughing at his own lame joke as Michelle rolled her eyes.

On June 3, the last day of the longest-ever primary season, Obama finally secured enough delegates to become the presumptive nominee. It was midnight before the Obama plane was wheels-up out of Minnesota, a state he needed to keep blue in November. The candidate had just given a rousing speech. If ever there was a time to party, this was it. "OK, pretty big night," Jim Margolis said to Obama. "You just locked up the nomination—how about a beer?" Obama started to say yes, then stopped. "We won't hit the ground until 3 in the morning, and I've got AIPAC first thing—I better not," he said. "OK, I'll have two," said Margolis. Obama was anxious about AIPAC, the American Israel Public Affairs Committee. Elderly Jewish voters in Florida—a key swing state in November—were telling reporters that they were leery of Obama, that some of them were not ready to vote for an African-American. The real campaign had begun.

Obama gets ready for his speech in Berlin, Germany, where as many as 200,000 people turned out to see him.

(Photo by Charles Ommanney / *Newsweek*)

FOUR

Going into Battle

McCain's inner circle altered the style, feel and direction of the campaign. The candidate's best hope was to bring down Obama.

MCCAIN WAS NOT A natural orator on the stump. He had trouble reading from a teleprompter, and he had an odd way of smiling at inappropriate times, flashing an expression that looked more like a frozen rictus than a friendly grin. During one early debate, he smiled broadly as he discussed crushing the enemy in Iraq. McCain could be moody, and he did not try very hard to disguise his moods. One of his advisers used the word "heady" to describe the candidate. He meant that his speaking style was easily swayed by his emotions. McCain could look hot or riled up (his traveling buddy Lindsey Graham particularly affected his moods, for better and for worse), or he could appear wooden, even sullen. McCain was bored by dreary presentations of his own polling data, but he could get agitated reading about other people's polls in the press.

His staff tried to keep away overstimulating distractions, but it was hopeless. During the campaign's low-budget period, when the candidate was traveling on the cut-rate airline Jet-Blue, he would get wound up watching political talk shows on the small video screen facing his seat.

Throughout the spring of 2008, McCain's uneven speaking style was a source of frustration to his aides. They knew how open and disarmingly honest he could be when he felt like it. But his stubborn integrity (or childish willfulness, depending on your point of view) was as much a liability as a virtue. When McCain didn't like the words he had been given to read, his inner Dennis the Menace would emerge, and he would sabotage his own speech.

McCain's subversive instincts had long shown up in his speaking style. Before the 2000 primary in South Carolina, when he spoke in favor of flying the Confederate flag over the state capitol, he would pull a piece of paper out of his pocket and read from it. It was obvious that he didn't really believe what he was saying and was ashamed of his pandering. His aides had trouble coaching him because the very act of telling him what to do could incite a rebellion. When distracted or restless, a not infrequent occasion, McCain could be tempted to play the high-school prankster. Once at a press availability in Kentucky he spotted a large woman, who was wearing a black T shirt embroidered with two bedazzling martini glasses, standing behind the photographers. He asked her to stand by him at the podium, where she might have a better view. "Is this OK?" he asked. "This is fi-ine!" the lady replied, but as she saw a sea of cameras and smirking reporters, she looked stunned and slightly embarrassed. She started to sidle away, and McCain asked, with mock forlornness, "You leaving me?"

In April, McCain gave a major "Service to America" speech at his alma mater, the U.S. Naval Academy. A select audience had been invited, and American flags provided a proud backdrop. But the crowd seemed tiny, dwarfed by the vast football stadium, and the flags flapped wildly and noisily. The morning sun shone on the teleprompter, so McCain couldn't read it and had to rely on a written speech. He trudged through his speech, but at one point when he looked up while turning a page, the wind caught a second page and turned it as well. McCain kept reading, but by the time he realized he had skipped a page it was too late. In the end it didn't really matter. His performance was so disjointed that the only people who really noticed were the reporters following the text on their laptops and BlackBerrys.

McCain should have enjoyed an advantage by securing the GOP nomination in March while Obama and Clinton ground on for three more months. But the press by and large ignored the GOP candidate, who was further hobbled by poor advance work as well as by his own listless or crabby performance. At times, McCain seemed to be amused by the haphazardness of his own organization. He would crack jokes about the "well-oiled machine we have here on this campaign." When the microphones kept dropping out during a Florida press conference, he declared, with mock outrage, "It's a plot!"

Perversely, part of McCain's problem behind the podium lay with his talented speechwriter and closest adviser, Mark Salter. The coauthor of his bestselling books, including *Faith of My Fathers* and *Why Courage Matters*, Salter idealized McCain and wanted him to be the heroic figure he was in his books. Salter wrote noble, eloquent speeches for McCain, high-flown words that evoked a spirit of selflessness and patriotism. Yet these sentiments—which McCain, more than any other candidate, personally embodied—sometimes sounded stilted and cringeworthy when they came from his mouth on the campaign trail. McCain may have actually believed the campaign myth that "Salter writes the way McCain thinks"; in any case, he wanted to be the hero that Salter had helped him become, and tried to sound like one. But if he became bored or his mind wandered, he read Salter's lofty words with all the conviction and gusto of a dutiful schoolboy reciting his Latin.

Salter and McCain had a close but complicated relationship. Salter was indebted to McCain; he had bought a second home in Maine with the money he earned from their books, and he had even met his wife, Diane, in the senator's office, where she had been a scheduler. At some level Salter worshiped McCain, but he knew not to fawn; indeed, he understood that the best way to get McCain's attention was to appear indifferent. Salter had the confidence to stand up to McCain—the relationship was more brotherly than father-son. Salter could imagine McCain's thoughts and supply his words, and he fancied that he knew him better than anyone. But he never really got inside McCain's head; no one did.

Traveling on a national presidential campaign can be exhilarating, but it is also exhausting, and it can be disorienting. Campaign aides can spend months far from home and family, living out of suitcases, eating junk food and drinking too much. The seats on the back half of the campaign plane are usually filled with Secret Service agents whose job it is to protect the candidate from being assassinated, and reporters whose job it is (or appears to be) to catch the candidate slipping up. No wonder that from time to time, campaign aides like to hit the hotel bar at night.

Salter's drinking buddy was Steve Schmidt. Early in the campaign, they would drink deep into the night, working themselves up about the awfulness of the press and the shallowness of Obama, whom they giddily mocked as "the One." (They were riffing off a Maureen Dowd column; with her sharp reporter's eye, the *New York Times*-woman had poked fun at Oprah Winfrey's adulation of Obama as "the One.") Egged on by Schmidt, Salter railed against the press for ignoring McCain and deifying Obama. "McCain goes to Iraq—they only make fun of him. Obama goes to Europe—three anchors and 200 other reporters go to chronicle the history-making Save America's Reputation Tour," Salter acidly remarked to a *Newsweek* reporter after getting stoked up night after night with Schmidt.

Salter and Schmidt were a bit of an odd couple. Though gruff and sarcastic, Salter was a humanist who was able to see reporters as human beings, even if he regarded them as tragically flawed, caught in a losing battle between idealism and cynicism. Schmidt preferred to see the world in black and white; individual reporters might be tolerable, even likable, but the press was simply the enemy. Salter had a temper, and it showed in angry e-mails telling off reporters (one such missive to a *Newsweek* editor concluded, "You're making this s——up"). Schmidt, when mad, became intense, prosecuting offenders carefully and deliberately.

Schmidt was a product of the Bush-Cheney '04 campaign. A midlevel staffer charged with running the rapid-response unit, Schmidt had been eager to be included in the exclusive "breakfast club" meetings run by Karl Rove, Bush's political mastermind. Schmidt's entree was his mastery of "oppo," shorthand in campaigns for their "opposition research" files on a rival's weakness. Nicknamed "the Bullet" by Rove for his shaved head and blunt manner, Schmidt had become a walking oppo-research book on John Kerry and the other Democratic candidates. Schmidt's working credo was what he called the Seven P's: Proper Prior Preparation Prevents Piss-Poor Performance.

RUNNING NEGATIVE CAMPAIGNS is as old as the republic (Jefferson slimed Adams), but in modern national campaigns, Republicans have been better at the game than Democrats. There is by now a well-thumbed playbook for defeating Democratic candidates. The original author was Richard Nixon, who, back in 1950, ran against Helen Gahagan Douglas for the U.S. Senate and succeeded in branding his opponent as a communist sympathizer by talking about her "pink underwear." Nixon had promised to avoid personal attacks (and thus earned the nickname "Tricky Dick");

he was adept at mixing high rhetoric with low blows. These tactics became a strategy in his appeal to the Silent Majority fearful of black crime and rioting students in 1968. The politics of fear were perfected by the legendary Republican operative Lee Atwater in the 1980s. The Atwater machine's *pièce de résistance* had been the Willie Horton ads, which suggested, not too subtly, that Democrat Michael Dukakis would be soft on crime because, as governor of Massachusetts, he had approved of a prison-furlough program that allowed a convicted rapist to rape again. Though Schmidt was hardly as devilish as Atwater, he understood the power of isolating some small, seemingly trivial weakness of the opponent—and bludgeoning it.

Schmidt resented being called a disciple of Rove by the press. He did not regard himself as a fearmonger or a practitioner of the dark arts, and indeed he had a sweet, playful side. He told funny stories about being scared of snakes at his California home, and he desperately missed his wife, son and daughter, with whom he had memorized the songs from the Disney fairy-tale movie *Enchanted*. After he had been portrayed as a calculating political-machine man in the 2004 *Newsweek* special election issue, a crestfallen Schmidt asked his friend Nicolle Wallace, Bush's communications director, "Is that really how people see me? The big, bald, mean guy?" Schmidt could be mock-tough. "I'm OK with a reign of terror starting now," he sternly told Salter when the campaign's logistical incompetence was becoming all too apparent to the press late in the spring of 2008. Then he turned to a *Newsweek* reporter and choked up with laughter. But he could also be severe and grimly focused. Whenever McCain had a rough day in the press, or Schmidt was running on a few hours' sleep after a late night at the bar with Salter, he would declare, throughout the day, "Fun Steve is dead."

At first Schmidt was not an easy fit with campaign manager Rick Davis. In the estimation of Davis, Schmidt suffered from attention-deficit disorder. Schmidt, to be sure, was not very good with columns of numbers (as a student, he had been unable to pass required math at the University of Delaware and had dropped out). But he was relentlessly disciplined and on message—two attributes the campaign sorely lacked. He spoke in declarative sentences, with a flat certainty, which appealed to McCain's fondness for stand-up guys and impulsive, let's-do-it instincts.

In early June, Schmidt took over control of day-to-day operations in the campaign. The press played the move as another major campaign shake-up. The last straw, the press reported, was a sour, poorly staged speech by McCain on June 3, the day Obama formally secured the Democratic nomination. McCain had looked like a grumpy old man. Actually, it was Schmidt who had ordered the sickly green backdrop that made the candidate look old and greenish-gray, and it was Schmidt who had told Salter and McCain to come out hard against Obama. Schmidt wasn't directly replacing Davis—McCain advisers were not so much shoved out as pushed to the side, and Davis retained the title of campaign manager, along with many of the responsibilities.

But Schmidt's ascension would profoundly alter the style, feel and fundamental direction of the campaign.

By his own account, Davis had wanted Schmidt to come back to headquarters to help run things. To Davis, it seemed that Schmidt and Salter and others like Charlie Black, a veteran Washington lobbyist who advised McCain, were off having fun on the campaign plane, a merry band of brothers, while he was stuck back at headquarters, overwhelmed by trying to ramp up McCain's cheapskate insurgency into a fully staffed presidential campaign. He needed Schmidt to take charge of the daily message and media operation. If that meant reining in the candidate as he wandered about cracking jokes and saying pretty much whatever came into his mind, so be it.

Still, Davis did not want to lose the spirit of the pirate ship. On March 1, as McCain was securing the nomination, a *Newsweek* reporter had asked Davis if the time had come to "trim down the pirate ship and become more of a cruise ship." No, Davis responded, "it'll always be a pirate ship. Not because of the size of it, but certainly because of the attitude of it. As long as John McCain's got the patch over the right eye, that ain't going away."

But it did. The last voyage of the pirate ship was called off before it ever left the dock. McCain genuinely loved informal give-and-take. He was fearless (maybe a little too much so) in a town-hall setting, fielding questions from ordinary citizens, or sitting around with reporters on the Straight Talk Express. In early June, he sent a letter to Obama inviting the Illinois senator to participate in a series of joint town-hall meetings. McCain had a romantic idea of traveling the country with a worthy opponent, engaged in a meaningful dialogue that would educate and challenge voters. The idea had been broached by Mark McKinnon, an old Bush adviser, who, in turn, had been inspired by an idea first floated by John F. Kennedy before his assassination in 1963. JFK had wanted to be seen with his likely Republican opponent, Barry Goldwater, because he thought he could beat him. Goldwater suggested they tour together before the 1964 election. It was a noble-seeming idea, and it might possibly have civilized and elevated the 2008 election. But it was not to be. McCain proposed debating every week until Election Day—some 20 weeks away. Obama's aides were wary of taking on the GOP candidate in forums that seemed to favor McCain's brash, conversational style. They counterproposed two "Lincoln-Douglas style" debates, where each candidate would give an hourlong speech and have a half hour for rebuttal, in addition to the traditional three debates in the fall. This format favored Obama, the orator. The Obamaites wanted the first debate on July 4.

McCain really believed his opponent would do the town halls with him and was disappointed by Obama's response. But his aides were outraged, or pretended to be. (One later confessed to a *Newsweek* reporter that they never expected Obama to say yes; they were just looking to take the moral high ground.) The Fourth of July, said Rick Davis, was "the worst viewing night of the year," and he told a reporter that the Obama response was "the most sarcastic thing I have ever heard anybody do." The Obama team, for its part, was indignant when the McCain team went to the press with its complaints before negotiating with Obama—or even replying to his counteroffer. Before long, the whole idea collapsed in recriminations.

McCain's inner circle was furious when the press appeared to give Obama a free pass or equally apportioned the blame. The press treatment of the whole affair deepened the perception among McCain's aides that the liberal media establishment was determined to get Obama elected. McCain was no longer the darling of the media, or so it appeared to Schmidt, Salter and Davis. That was the message they wanted to impress on the candidate. Reporters, they told McCain, don't want to debate you about the great issues of the day. They just want "gotcha" stories. The McCain advisers were particularly leery of the "embedded" TV-network producers, who carried small cameras everywhere to capture every campaign moment. Their network bosses back in New York were salivating for footage of McCain stumbling, Schmidt concluded. Salter, still simmering over the *New York Times* story about McCain and the female lobbyist, agreed. Salter felt betrayed; after all that access, the press just wanted to "get" McCain. The two began warning McCain not to speak to reporters. "When he goes to the back of the bus, Schmidt and I say, 'Danger, danger, not the same press corps. They want to make news today, and the easiest way to make news is if it comes at your expense,'" Salter told a *Newsweek* reporter. Schmidt, Salter and Davis spent hours working themselves up over the perceived unfairness in coverage. McCain aides began joking that NBC, mother ship of MSNBC's avowedly liberal anchorman Keith Olbermann, had become "National Barack Channel," while Davis scoffed to the *Newsweek* reporter that "*The New York*

Times has become a 527"—a provision in the tax code regulating groups that buy ads to push pet causes, usually with the effect of promoting one candidate or another.

McCain was nonplused about the end of his honeymoon with the press. He liked hanging around with reporters; they were his friends, or at least his sparring partners. (He enjoyed the challenge; "he never met an interview he didn't think he could beat," said his spokesperson, Jill Hazelbaker.) McCain would want to head back to the reporters' section of the plane, and Davis would pull him back. "No, no, no, I want them around me," McCain would say, referring to the reporters. "No, no, no, they're screwing you," Davis would retort.

At McCain's insistence, his new campaign plane in the summer of 2008 had been fitted with a large bench-style couch, to re-create the space on the Straight Talk Express bus, where the candidate had spent hours jawing on the record with reporters, half a dozen or so at a time. But reporters were never asked to sit there. McCain did not look happy about being kept on a tight leash, as least as far as reporters could tell from a distance. ("It was like withdrawal," Lindsey Graham conceded to a *Newsweek* reporter.) Around reporters, McCain sometimes looked like a sheepish teenager who has been told by his parents that he has to stop seeing a girl. At a stop in Wisconsin, reporters watched while McCain drank coffee with a delegate. The candidate looked up and made eye contact with the reporters. "How are you guys today?" he said, smiling. Before anyone could say anything, campaign aides swooped in and began ushering reporters from the room. When one reporter tried to talk to McCain, he looked up expectantly and seemed about to say something. "Senator, can I . . ." the reporter began. An advance man stepped in. "Thank you, let's go," the staffer said.

McCain's almost willful tendency to step all over his scripted lines exasperated his aides. Before Obama left on a widely anticipated overseas trip in mid-July, the McCain camp tried to orchestrate a counterattack. Jill Hazelbaker went on Fox TV's morning show to mock Obama. "Let's drop the pretense that this is a fact-finding trip and call it what it is: the first-of-its-kind campaign rally overseas." She called the trip "one giant photo opportunity." But McCain promptly told reporters that he disagreed with Hazelbaker and that he would speak to her about it. McCain said he was "glad" that Obama was going to Iraq and Afghanistan to see for himself. Hazelbaker was so upset that she did not come to work the next day and refused to take McCain's apologetic phone calls. Schmidt told the candidate in no uncertain terms that he had to change. McCain, for once, seemed to get the message.

On July 24, after touring the Middle East and Europe, meeting with foreign leaders and generally impressing the American and international press, Obama spoke to a huge crowd in Berlin. His campaign was eager to strike echoes of John F. Kennedy traveling to Berlin in 1963, the vibrant young leader thrilling the world with his defiance of Soviet communism. An advance team looked into the possibility of Obama's speaking at the Brandenburg Gate, near the place where Ronald Reagan had challenged the Soviets to "tear down this wall!" in the last days of the cold war. But Obama vetoed the site. He did not want to appear "presumptuous," he told David Axelrod, by speaking at a site normally reserved for heads of state. Still, he ended up speaking on a raised platform before the soaring Victory Column, not too far from the Brandenburg Gate, and the effect was both dramatic and grand.

Sen. Lindsey Graham was watching on TV. McCain's friend, who had sharp political instincts, saw an opportunity. As he later recalled, he thought, "Oh, boy," as he reached for the phone to call McCain. "Look at this!" he exclaimed to the candidate, who was also watching. "Who the hell does this guy think he is? And who are all those Germans, and what are they cheering about?" To Graham, Obama's speech was all about Obama, grandstanding for a bunch of foreigners.

Other McCain advisers were having similar thoughts and inspirations. That weekend, the senior strategy team met at a hotel near McCain's house in Phoenix to ponder how to turn Obama's big moment against him. McCain, his wife and Graham joined at the end of the meeting to see what they had come up with.

Schmidt took the lead. Obama was flying so high that McCain's guns could barely reach him, he said. So the answer was . . . make him fly a little higher, until the voters saw that he really was nothing more than a hot-air balloon. "This guy is acting like a celebrity," Schmidt said. "He is a celebrity. Only celebrities draw 200,000 people. Presidents do, too, but he's not a president. He's the biggest celebrity in the world. OK, let's give him that. Let him have that. But then we get to ask, do you want a celebrity running the country?"

Graham immediately perked up. "That's great!" he exclaimed. McCain nodded. "Yeah," he said. Schmidt quickly got to work on an ad. On July 30, the "celebrity" ad went up and was quickly flashed around the country on news shows and YouTube. "He's the biggest celebrity in the world," a breathy announcer declares, while images of Obama's Berlin speech are juxtaposed with shots of Paris Hilton and Britney Spears.

Most pundits huffed at the ad as trivial and a cheap shot. But it dominated the news cycle for several days, something McCain had failed to do for months. Obama didn't get much of a bounce from his trip, despite the heavy, overwhelmingly admiring press coverage. The ad had helped stall Obama's momentum and, with some voters, raise doubts about his depth of experience. Schmidt's status rose: his chippy, in-your-face attack mode seemed to work.

Still, McCain's own adman, Mike Hudome, was unsettled. He told a *Newsweek* reporter that Paris Hilton and Britney Spears were not his style. Friends and colleagues would stop him and say, "Hey, Mike, the celebrity spot?" Hudome would hasten to tell them that the spot was all Schmidt's doing. Hudome liked Schmidt, but he felt bad about the direction of the campaign; under Schmidt, it was being run more like a traditional political campaign, going negative and sticking to the sound bites. He worried that the campaign was forfeiting "the real McCain maverick message." And yet he had to concede the ad worked.

McCain himself seemed grouchy and unhappy on the campaign trail. He was doing fewer town-hall meetings, and his aides, upset when no one laughed at the candidate's tried-and-true jokes at one particularly sorry affair in Belleville, Mich., decided they'd better start packing the hall with Mc-Cainiacs. (The audience was full of undecided and skeptical voters; the campaign had been trying to make a point with the press and Obama by daring to plunge the candidate into true arenas of democracy—i.e., before unscreened voters.) Before long, McCain's "town halls" were almost as tame as George W. Bush's in 2004, when the president spoke to by-invitation-only crowds.

McCain chafed at his handlers from time to time. But as one close aide explained to a *Newsweek* reporter, he did not mind sudden course shifts in his campaign. He was a fighter pilot, an improviser, not a "steady as she goes" sailor. All through his political career, he had been willing to tack away from the fleet. He was regarded as quirky and unpredictable by his stodgier, more conventionally partisan colleagues. McCain may have bridled at doing fewer town-hall meetings or cutting off the press, but he was able to reconcile any qualms about going negative by regarding change—in this case, a tougher, sharper-edged approach—as not only necessary but desirable. "There aren't very many politicians who are instinctively as good as John at saying, 'I got it. New campaign? No problem,'" said a close adviser. "His whole career is all over the map. This is not like Ronald Reagan—'Here's what I believe, I've never changed in 20 years.' This is John McCain, so change is a little bit quicker. He's like, 'OK.'"

McCain did not, in any case, resist taking a few jabs at Obama. McCain did not really respect his opponent. He can

Senator Obama works on his victory speech backstage with Michelle, Sasha (left), and Malia (right) in Des Moines, Iowa, on January 3, 2008.

(Photo by Charles Ommanney/*Newsweek*)

Hillary and Chelsea Clinton watch as returns come in on March 4, 2008—election night for the primaries in Columbus, Ohio.

(Photo by Jonathan Torgovnik/*Newsweek*)

Debbie Blevins of Warfield, Kentucky, smiles after being invited to the podium by John McCain during McCain's "It's Time for Action" campaign tour.

(Photo by Mary Altaffer / AP)

Obama and his staff members pass around a basketball backstage at a town hall meeting in Fairfax County, Virginia. (Photo by Charles Ommanney / *Newsweek*)

Shortly before being officially named the Democratic presidential nominee, Obama works on his convention speech. (Photo by Charles Ommanney / *Newsweek*)

Obama on his six-day "Road to Change" bus tour through Pennsylvania.

(Photo by Charles Ommanney / *Newsweek*)

Obama greets students after a prayer meeting with Hispanic Evangelical Ministers in Brownsville, Texas.

Obama watches Hillary Clinton addressing the Democratic National Convention at a Democratic supporters' group.

(Photo by Charles Ommanney / *Newsweek*)

Malia and Sasha Obama sit in the holding room on day four of the Democratic National Convention. (Photo by Charles Ommanney / *Newsweek*)

Joe Biden squeezes Sasha's cheeks backstage at the Democratic National Convention. (Photo by Charles Ommanney / *Newsweek*)

Obama and Biden chat with senior advisor David Axelrod before taking off in the campaign plane. (Photo by Charles Ommanney / *Newsweek*)

The Obama family backstage at a rally near the Iowa state capitol building.

(Photo by Charles Ommanney/*Newsweek*)

Cindy and Meghan McCain in one of their hotel rooms. The hotel embroidered all of their names on their pillows to make it feel more like home.

(Photo by Heather Brand/Aurora)

Sarah Palin holds her son, Trig, and checks her BlackBerry backstage at a rally in Dayton, Ohio. (Photo by Heather Brand/Aurora)

Cindy McCain sits between senior advisor Mark Salter and John McCain in a Pittsburgh bar. (Photo by Khue Bui/*Newsweek*)

John and Cindy McCain cooking at their cabin in Sedona, Arizona.

(Photo by Heather Brand/Aurora)

Senior McCain advisors Steve Duprey (left) and Mark Salter (right) play "Rocky" during a McCain rally. (Photo by Khue Bui/*Newsweek*)

McCain pulls up to a rally in his "Straight Talk Express" bus.

(Photo by Khue Bui/*Newsweek*)

McCain at a town hall meeting on September 17, 2008, in Grand Rapids, Michigan.

Obama's final rally on November 3, 2008, in Manassas, Virginia.

The McCains take the stage in Phoenix on election night, where Senator McCain gave a gracious concession speech that saluted the historical import of Obama's victory and blamed himself for the loss.

(Photo by Khue Bui / *Newsweek*)

"It has been a long time coming," Obama said in his victory speech in Chicago, "but tonight . . . change has come to America."

(Photo by Charles Ommanney / *Newsweek*)

be forgiving, but he can also hold a grudge, and for him politics is deeply personal. He felt that he had been betrayed by Obama in the Senate, and that Obama, as he put it, lacked guts (a critical test to the macho McCain). McCain's essential world view, bred into him by his Navy-admiral father and grandfather, is that of a warrior. In his bestsellers, McCain made clear that the personal quality he extols above all others—even courage—is honor. Over time, egged on by his subordinates, he came to believe that Obama was a nice enough young man, but somehow lacking in this most noble of warrior virtues.

McCain was fairly bipartisan in his likes and dislikes; he was just as willing to denounce a Republican pork-barreler as a Democrat, and he would gladly work with Democrats he could trust. Indeed, in *Worth the Fighting For*, he recounts his close friendship with, and deep respect for, the late Morris Udall, a liberal Democrat from Arizona. McCain was always ready for friends across the aisle. At first he thought he had found one in the young Obama. As a freshly elected U.S. senator in 2005, Obama had approached McCain and told the senior senator that he didn't want to be a party hack—that he wanted to be more like him. "McCain is always on the lookout for guys like that," recalled Salter.

McCain decided to ask Obama to collaborate with him on ethics reform. McCain was part of a bipartisan group with Sen. Rick Santorum, a conservative Pennsylvania Republican. Obama showed up at one meeting of the Santorum group—but never again. (According to Santorum, McCain gave Obama a "syrupy" welcome when he walked into the room.) Obama had publicly stated that he was open to working with

Republicans on ethics reform, and he had privately assured McCain of his cooperation. But then he backed out, without first calling McCain. Salter assumed that Obama had been yanked back by Harry Reid, Democrat from Nevada, the fiercely partisan Senate majority leader who did not like freshmen wandering off the reservation.

What really irked McCain and Salter was the way Obama backed out. He wrote a somewhat formal letter to McCain, thanking him for the chance to participate in the Santorum working group but saying he preferred his own party's legislation. Before the letter made it to McCain, it was leaked to the press, probably by someone in Reid's office. Salter was incensed when he learned of Obama's intentions by reading the newspaper. He fumed: How dare this junior senator throw McCain's generosity back in his face! And do it so publicly!

McCain was also miffed, and he instructed Salter to ghostwrite a letter back to Obama: "I would like to apologize to you for assuming that your private assurances to me regarding your desire to cooperate in our efforts to negotiate bipartisan lobbying reform legislation were sincere," Salter's draft began, dripping with contempt, and just grew more sarcastic: "I understand how important the opportunity to lead your party's effort to exploit this issue must seem to a freshman Senator, and I hold no hard feelings over your earlier disingenuousness. Again, I have been around long enough to appreciate that in politics the public interest isn't always a priority for every one of us."

Salter would later say that the tone of the letter was perhaps more bitter than McCain intended (though McCain did sign the letter). Obama, for his part, seemed genuinely startled by McCain's acid-tipped arrow. He wrote McCain, "The fact that you have questioned my sincerity and my desire to put aside politics for the public interest is regrettable but does not in any way diminish my deep respect for you or my willingness to find a bipartisan solution to this problem."

Obama further alienated McCain on the immigration issue. McCain took great political risks on immigration, defying the GOP faithful who wanted to build a wall across the Mexican border and arrest and detain illegal immigrants. Working with Ted Kennedy and a bipartisan group, McCain came up with compromise legislation to create a guest-worker program. Obama asked to join the group. The senators agreed to hang together to vote against amendments from both the right and the left. Some very conservative senators honored the agreement, voting against conservative amendments—but Obama did not, voting in favor of a number of liberal amendments. After one meeting, Kennedy chewed Obama out for his fickleness. (Months later, asked by a colleague why he had endorsed Obama for president, Kennedy gave a one-word answer: "Caroline.") With his aides, McCain initially took a forgiving tone toward Obama. When Salter ranted to his boss that Obama was being spineless on immigration reform, McCain responded, "He's a rookie, he's a rookie. Maybe he'll grow into something." But on the campaign trail in late July 2008, with the election less than four months away and McCain hanging in close behind the front runner, when Schmidt and others pressed to go negative and mock Obama, McCain did not hold them back.

There was a notable lack of diversity at the top of the Obama campaign, a situation that Obama himself occasionally complained about, though not so strongly that anything was done to add on more minorities. Hillary Clinton had put two black women (campaign manager Maggie Williams and chief of staff Cheryl Mills) in charge, replacing her first campaign manager, Patti Solis Doyle, who is Hispanic. More gay men found high-level positions on her staff as well.

After Clinton bowed out in June and Obama's staff bulked up for the general election, one newcomer, settling into the open workspace at 233 North Michigan Avenue, noticed something else different from Hillaryland. The campaign veteran took note of the "No-Drama Obama" atmosphere, but observed to a *Newsweek* reporter, "There's drama in Obama. People just whisper, not yell." David Plouffe, Obama's campaign manager, ordered his staff to welcome the Clinton refugees (reportedly threatening that if they did not, "I will hunt you down"). There was a slight hitch when Clinton's top fundraisers were folded into Obama's finance committee. According to one of Obama's moneymen, the Clinton people wanted to know what their job titles would be and were taken aback when they were informed that the Obama fundraisers had no titles. (Several wealthy women who had raised money for Clinton decided instead to raise money for McCain; one of them, Lynn Forester de Rothschild, later said that Obama was an "elitist" who talked down to "rednecks.")

The former Clinton adviser noticed that the atmosphere felt different from Hillaryland in another way. "People walk around there," the Clintonista said, gesturing to the tower on Michigan Avenue, "thinking there is *no possible* way he can lose." The adviser came from an alternate universe, one with a healthier sense of impending disaster. "I worked in the Clinton White House," the adviser recalled, "and we assumed that if something *could* go wrong, it *would* go wrong."

By early August, however, the true believers in the Obama campaign were beginning to have a few doubts. They were bothered that McCain's "celebrity" ad had apparently penetrated Obama's image armor, even though their own internal polls still seemed to be holding up. To the former Clinton aide, it seemed, some of the top Obamaites were operating under the illusion that they had weathered the worst from Hillary Clinton. "They live in a world where they think Hillary was the meanest she could be," the aide told a *Newsweek* reporter. The Clintonista believed that Hillary had held back—noting that when Hillary was asked in a debate if Obama was electable, she said yes, which was not what she was saying privately.

T HERE WERE SOME OBAMAITES bracing for the worst. Media man Jim Margolis took notice of the fact that McCain had announced that he would not "referee" between the 527s, the independent-expenditure groups. If there was any racist or truly low-road attack on Obama, it was likely to come from the 527s, which are prohibited by law from communicating with presidential campaigns—and are thus free to sling mud with impunity. It had been a 527, Swift

Boat Veterans for Truth, that did the most harm to John Kerry in 2004 by questioning his war record in Vietnam. The Internet was constantly buzzing with viral assassins who spread rumors that Obama was a Muslim, that he had attended a madrassa and that there was a video of Michelle making a crack about "Whitey." "It's a lie," Margolis told a *Newsweek* reporter in June. "We're going to be aggressive." That same day, the Obama campaign launched a Web site called Fightthesmears.com to rebut the various falsehoods.

Obama's own approach was, as usual, to play it cool. In April, when Clinton was beginning to push the line by saying that she stood for "hardworking, white Americans," Obama told a crowd in Raleigh, N.C., "When you're running for president, then you've got to expect it, and you've kind of got to let it . . ." He paused, shrugged and made a brushing motion with his right hand, as if flicking some dust off his right shoulder, then his left. The crowd, which included many African-Americans, burst into surprised laughter and applause, and many stood to cheer as Obama gave a self-satisfied smile and an exaggerated nod, and then said, "That's what you gotta do." He was playing off the popular song "Dirt Off Your Shoulder" by the hip-hop artist Jay-Z. ("If you feelin' like a pimp nigga, go and brush your shoulders off/Ladies is pimps too, go and brush your shoulders off/Niggaz is crazy baby, don't forget that boy told you/Get that dirt off your shoulder.")

With McCain's "celebrity" ad, the Obama camp saw a warning shot. Obama's aides did not think the McCain campaign would ever explicitly play the race card, but by raising questions about Obama's experience, McCain's message makers hoped to fuel fears that Obama was not trustworthy and that he was somehow "other" from mainstream voters, particularly working-class older whites. At least that's the way it looked to Obama's spinmeisters, so they began feeding Obama lines aimed at inoculating voters. In Springfield, Mo., on July 30, the same day the "celebrity" ad first aired, Obama told the crowd, "So nobody really thinks that Bush or McCain have [sic] the real answer for the challenges we face, so what they're going to try to do is make you scared of me. You know, he's not patriotic enough. He's got a funny name. You know, he doesn't look like all those other presidents on those dollar bills, you know. He's risky." Obama repeated the same message at two more stops along the trail of mostly white voters in Missouri.

At McCain headquarters, righteous indignation was the order of the day. Political campaigners rarely lack for excuses to describe the opposition as wicked and evil, but the race issue seemed to strike a particularly sensitive chord among the McCain advisers. Republicans as well as Democrats learned (or perhaps over-learned) the lesson of the Swift Boat attacks on Kerry in 2004: don't wait to hit back. At McCain headquarters, voices were raised against Obama for daring to suggest that McCain was using racial innuendo. It was decided to play a little jujitsu and have Rick Davis accuse Obama of playing the race card himself. "Barack Obama has played the race card, and played it from the bottom of the deck," Davis declared in a press release.

That afternoon, Davis did a phone interview with Andrea Mitchell of MSNBC to defend his comments and the "celebrity" ad. "Explain to me, Rick, how is what he said playing the race card?" Mitchell asked in a skeptical tone. Davis accused the Obama campaign of telling reporters and liberal bloggers that McCain's attacks "had racial overtones." Mitchell challenged Davis about the increasingly negative feel of the campaign, and the conversation grew testy. Davis regarded Mitchell's tone as condescending, and he grew so hot arguing with her that he forgot he was on a phone call being played over the air to hundreds of thousands of MSNBC viewers. When he hung up the phone, he barged out of his office to clear his head, and he was startled to receive a standing ovation from his staff.

On the campaign trail, McCain was asked about Davis's "race card" remarks. McCain looked uneasy and tepidly endorsed his campaign manager's remarks, but said that the campaign needed to return to debating the issues. After a brief kerfuffle, the press let the matter drop. Reporters are as uncomfortable as the politicians they cover about discussing race.

Still, among the punditocracy and on the blogs, there was some chatter. As they sat around in greenrooms waiting to go on cable-TV talk shows, pundits and reporters engaged in some cynical speculation. Had the McCain campaign attacked Obama for playing the race card precisely to bring up the whole question of race? To remind voters that race was an issue—the elephant in the room? There was a certain logic to these suspicions. In many polls, the generic Democrat defeated the generic Republican by 10 points or more, simply because voters were ready for a change after eight years of Republican rule. Yet Obama and McCain, by midsummer 2008, were essentially tied. Why wasn't Obama doing better? McCain's supporters argued that McCain outperformed the generic Republican candidate because he was a maverick attractive to independent voters and because he was a more experienced leader than Obama. But some polling experts suspected (though they couldn't quite prove, since polling on race is so difficult) that Obama was held back by the color of his skin.

Given the national mood, McCain was going to have a difficult time persuading a majority of Americans to vote Republican come November. Standard procedure among political consultants faced with such reality is to go negative. Negative ads can depress the candidate's standing, that's true. But if done right, they bring down the opponent's standing even more. Hence, McCain's best (perhaps only) hope was to bring down Obama.

There was no question but that Schmidt & Co. were going negative, and that McCain was somewhat grudgingly going along. But McCain's advisers took violent exception to any suggestion that they were using race in any way to undercut Obama. Their touchiness on the subject had a whiff of "the lady doth protest too much," and some of the anger at reporters was calculated, intended to scare the press away from writing stories that even hinted that McCain was using the old Republican playbook. But they were determined not to do or say anything that might be deemed racist. At one point they considered mocking Obama as "the One" with an ad showing footage of him onstage with Oprah Winfrey. But the idea was nixed—it might be misinterpreted. There was genuine frustration on the part of McCain's aides, who griped that they would get blamed by the press for playing on racial fears no matter what they did. They heatedly pointed out to reporters that McCain had denounced a Republican operative who used racial innuendo in an ad in North Carolina, and that McCain had repeatedly expressed his distaste for race baiting in political campaigns.

McCAIN WAS SINCERE. He did not want to win by playing on racial anxiety. He had too vivid a memory of being smeared in South Carolina in 2000. His wife, Cindy, had an even more searing recollection. She personally blamed Karl Rove, Bush's political guru, for unleashing the old Lee Atwater attack machine, using anonymous smear artists to spread around leaflets suggesting that her adopted daughter, Bridget, was the love child of John McCain and a black prostitute. Rove always vigorously denied any such thing, and the link was never proved. McCain, who prided himself on his sense of forgiveness, told friends that he was willing to get along with Rove and move on. But Cindy never did. At a private gathering in Aspen, Colo., in the summer of 2007, a friend asked Cindy whether she would stab Rove in the back if he walked by. "No," she answered, "I'd stab him in the front."

To the casual visitor, the New Media department at Obama headquarters seemed at once ultrahip and painfully earnest, a touchy-feely, emo sort of place where people talk about saving their souls and use lefty academic jargon like "agency." One reporter described the sentiment toward the candidate as a sort of "Lincoln 2.0." The frat brothers over in Communications liked to joke about whether the geeks in New Media were still virgins.

When it came to what they actually did, however, the nerds of New Media were cold realists. "We never do something just because it's cool," the campaign's official blogger, Sam Graham-Felsen, told a *Newsweek* reporter. "We're always nerdily getting something out of it." He showed off the Obama '08 iPhone application. With its deep Obama blues, correct fonts and glassy graphics, it looked like an electronic bauble for the well-heeled voter. Closer inspection revealed a sophisticated data-mining operation. Tap the top button, "call friends," and the software would take a peek at your phone book and rearrange it in the order that the campaign was targeting states, so that friends who had, say, Colorado or Virginia area codes would appear at the top. With another tap, the Obama supporter could report back essential data for a voter canvass ("left message," "not interested," "already voted," etc.). It all went into a giant database for Election Day.

Early that summer, the campaign made the unorthodox decision to announce its vice presidential pick via text messages sent directly to supporters. It wasn't just a trick to do something flashy with technology and attract media attention. The point was to collect voters' cell-phone numbers for later contact during voter registration and get-out-the-vote efforts. Thanks to the promotion, the campaign's list of cell-phone numbers increased several-fold to more than 1 million. (Among the registrees: one Beau Biden, son of Joe.)

"I don't care about online energy and enthusiasm just for the sake of online energy and enthusiasm," said Chris Hughes, head of New Media's social networking. "It's about making money, making phone calls, embedding video or having video forwarded to friends." There was nothing starry-eyed about Hughes, who had been the Harvard roommate and later partner of Facebook founder Mark Zuckerberg and made his first millions before he was 24. His goal was to make old techniques—like call centers and getting polling information to voters—more efficient. "When computer applications really take off, they take something people have always done and just make it easier for them to do it," he said. "And maybe bigger."

During the primaries, the sight was familiar at vast Obama rallies. Before the candidate appeared, a campaign official would come onstage to urge audience members to pull out their cell phones to call or text their friends and neighbors. By the thousands, people of all ages would spread the electronic word—and dollars and votes would follow. Joe Rospars, the director of Obama's New Media, noted, "We didn't invent the idea of our supporters calling one another. We just made it a lot easier." Rospars had written a blog for the Howard Dean campaign in 2004. Under Rospars, the Obama campaign had basically perfected Dean's 1.0 tactics with an important twist. Dean was all about creating a national network, but in Iowa he failed to build a true grass-roots campaign. In Obamaland, where the sayings of Saul Alinsky resonated ("think globally, act locally"), the emphasis was local—neighbor to neighbor, friend to friend, family to family. Joe Trippi, the unorthodox political genius who created the Dean Internet juggernaut, often said that if the Dean campaign was like the Wright Brothers at Kitty Hawk, then Obama was the Apollo program—in other words, in one cycle skipping over commercial aviation, jet travel and supersonic transport to go straight to the moon. (Asked about this analogy, Rospars replied evenly, "Not really, if you consider that Kitty Hawk was a successful flight, as compared to something that blew up on the f——ing launchpad.")

The power of the Obama operation could be measured: doubling the turnout at the Iowa caucuses, raising twice as much money as any other candidate in history, organizing volunteers by the millions. (In Florida alone: 65 offices, paid staff of 350, active e-mail list of 650,000, 25,000 volunteers on any weekend day.) The ultimate test would come Nov. 4. In the meantime, there were indications of a great storm brewing. At the end of August, as Hurricane Gustav threatened the coast of Texas, the Obama campaign called the Red Cross to say it would be routing donations to it via the Red Cross home page. *Get your servers ready—our guys can be pretty nuts*, Team Obama said. *Sure, sure, whatever*, the Red Cross responded. *We've been through 9/11, Katrina, we can handle it*. The surge of Obama dollars crashed the Red Cross Web site in less than 15 minutes.

Senator McCain and Governor Sarah Palin attend a rally in Fairfax, Virginia, on September 10, 2008. (Photo by Khue Bui/*Newsweek*)

FIVE

Center Stage

*Obama's aides worried the Clintons might
steal the show. McCain revved up his campaign
with an impulsive choice—Sarah Palin.*

IN MIDSUMMER, THE OBAMA campaign's computers were
attacked by a virus. The campaign's tech experts spotted
it and took standard precautions, such as putting in a fire-
wall. At first, the campaign figured it was a routine "phishing"
attack, using common methods. Or so it seemed. In fact, the
campaign had been the target of sophisticated foreign cyber-
espionage.

The next day, the Obama headquarters had two visitors:
from the FBI and the Secret Service. "You have a problem
way bigger than what you understand," said an FBI agent.
"You have been compromised, and a serious amount of files
have been loaded off your system." The Feds were cryptic
and did not answer too many questions. But the next day,
Obama campaign chief David Plouffe heard from White
House chief of staff Josh Bolten. "You have a real problem,"

Bolten told the Obama aide. "It's way bigger than you guys think and you have to deal with it."

By late afternoon the campaign's chief technology officer, Michael Slaby, was on the phone with the FBI field agent who was running the investigation out of Los Angeles. Slaby was told that the hackers had been moving documents out of Obama's system at a rapid rate. Potentially, Obama's entire computer network had been compromised.

The campaign brought in a top tech-security firm to scrub its system. On Aug. 18 an Obama official was summoned to FBI headquarters in Chicago for a briefing, only to be told that the White House had ordered the FBI not to give the briefing. The Obama official asked why, and was told that three hours earlier the Feds had learned that the McCain campaign had been compromised as well.

The security firm retained by the Obama campaign was finally able to remove the virus. (The campaign's fundraising records were kept on a different computer system and were never compromised.) On Aug. 20 the Obama campaign got its briefing from the FBI. The Obama team was told that its system had been hacked by a "foreign entity." The official would not say which "foreign entity," but indicated that U.S. intelligence believed that both campaigns had been the target of political espionage by some country—or foreign organization—that wanted to look at the evolution of the Obama and McCain camps on policy issues, information that might be useful in any negotiations with a future Obama or McCain administration. There was no suggestion that terrorists were involved; technical experts hired by the

Obama campaign speculated that the hackers were Russian or Chinese.

Obama himself was briefed, and his personal laptop was examined and found not to have been hacked. The Obama campaign took steps to better secure its computer system, including encrypting any documents used by the policy and transition teams. The Feds assured the Obama team that it had not been hacked by its political opponents, which was sort of reassuring. A senior McCain official confirmed to *Newsweek* that the campaign had been hacked and that the FBI had become involved. White House and FBI officials had no comment.

To David Axelrod, the stretch of August between Obama's triumphal tour abroad and the Democratic convention were "lost weeks." Looking back after the convention, Obama's chief strategist felt that the campaign had been in a "rut." Though the campaign publicly scoffed at McCain's "celebrity" ad as a bit of desperate fluff on the part of the McCainiacs, the more honest Obama advisers conceded that Obama had been knocked a little off stride, made more cautious. Axelrod decided to tone down the rock-star aspect of the campaign. The candidate was no longer scheduled into mega-rallies but rather performed at smaller, more-subdued events. Axelrod was a little uneasy about the coming Democratic convention in Denver. The campaign had already declared that Obama would address a football stadium full of supporters in Denver on the last night. The intention was to mimic John F. Kennedy, who in 1960 had departed the crowded convention hall to deliver his acceptance speech under the lights at the massive Los Angeles Coliseum. (The Obamaites also wanted to use the event to create a giant phone bank—everyone who attended was supposed to use their cell phones to call friends and family. Extra cell towers were brought in to accommodate the avalanche of calls and texting.) At Invesco Field in Denver, the production staff of the Democratic National Committee proposed erecting enormous white columns on either side of the podium with all sorts of lights and adornments. To Axelrod, the whole setup looked like an over-the-top version of ancient Greece—or, more likely, a scene set from the movie *Star Wars*—and he asked for something more modest and sober, simple but presidential. The designers came back with some white columns that vaguely resembled the arcade between the West Wing and the White House, still a little presumptuous, perhaps, but better than trying to re-create Mount Olympus.

THE OBAMA CAMPAIGN HAD always prided itself in staying away from the Washington hothouse of party hacks and lobbyists. But the nominating conventions are traditionally giant celebrations of the party establishment. Inevitably, there was some tension between Democratic regulars and the Obama insurgents on the road to Denver. Delegates and congressmen, normally showered with free tickets, were allotted relatively few in order to make room for grass-roots organizers. The freeze on freebies added to a chorus of complaints from Capitol Hill and the K Street Corridor: the Obama campaign wasn't listening, wasn't paying attention, wasn't seeking their advice—all of which was essentially true. The campaign did have Peter Rouse, who had been a top aide to Tom Daschle, the former Senate majority leader and close adviser to Obama. Rouse half-jokingly referred to himself as a "fixer." He proposed an elaborate outreach program to members of Congress, but the idea was rejected as too cumbersome and not really necessary. As one top adviser explained it, "Everyone loves a winner." If Obama won, all would be forgiven, the adviser said. And if he lost, well, it wouldn't matter. The Obama campaign did not want to get caught up in trying to satisfy all the interest groups that make up the modern Democratic Party—the one that had lost seven of the last 10 presidential elections. The John Kerry campaign set up elaborate liaison offices dedicated to ethnic groups, organized labor, groups for the disabled, for women, for gays and lesbians. Somewhat grudgingly, the Obama campaign agreed to have a single staffer devoted to each of these constituencies, but later decided the whole thing was a waste of manpower and dispersed the interest-group liaisons to go work in the field on get-out-the-vote operations.

There was some nervousness that the Clintons, with an eye on 2012, might try to steal the show, perhaps by demanding a noisy floor vote that would show how close Hillary had come to winning the nomination. The Obamaites figured that the Clintons could be counted on to do just enough to say that they *tried* to help Obama—but maybe not so much that he won in November. The Obama staff was petrified because nobody had seen a copy of Bill Clinton's speech, recalled Michael Sheehan, the veteran

Democratic speech coach. There were two possible explanations: one, that Clinton planned to say something controversial that he didn't want to share beforehand; and, two, that Clinton was continually rewriting his speech. Knowing Clinton's work habits, Sheehan assured them it was the latter.

In truth, Hillary Clinton was on better terms with John McCain than she was with Barack Obama. The former First Lady and the four-term senator from Arizona had downed shots together on Senate junkets; they regarded each other as grizzled veterans of the political wars and shared a certain disdain for Obama as flashy and callow. In early June, on the night she officially lost the Democratic nomination, Hillary had enjoyed a long and friendly phone conversation with McCain. When Hillary finally did meet with Obama at the home of Sen. Dianne Feinstein a few days later, she told Obama that she did not want to go through a full-scale vetting for vice president unless he was serious about choosing her. The vetting process was onerous, requiring very full financial disclosure, and even included questions about romantic and marital indiscretions. As the financial crisis deepened in the summer, Eric Holder, Obama's chief veep vetter, added more questions about mortgages and problematic financial deals.

Obama was not inclined to choose Hillary, not so much because she had been his sometime bitter rival on the campaign trail, but because of her husband. "You don't just get Hillary, you get Bill," said a top Obama adviser. The Obamaites had benefited from Bill Clinton as a loose cannon in the primary campaign. They did not want to be wounded by him in the general election. Still, from time to time, as Hillary's name came up in veep discussions, and Obama's advisers gave all the reasons she should be kept off the ticket, Obama would stop and ask, "Are we sure?" He needed to be convinced one more time that the Clintons would do more harm than good.

The caution that had settled over the campaign in the wake of the "celebrity" ad crept into Obama's veep deliberations. Obama's personal favorite was Tim Kaine, the young governor of Virginia, a reformer who could win red-state votes. Like Obama, Kaine had come from a poor background but graduated from Harvard Law School. "I really like this guy," Obama said of Kaine. The one-term Virginia governor was the easiest to vet—"He's as pure as this," said Holder, waving a blank white sheet of paper. But, with the Republicans banging on about Obama as too inexperienced, Kaine was deemed to be too risky a choice. Early in the process, Obama announced, "I'm leaning toward Biden," the six-term senator from Delaware. Joe Biden had experience as chairman of the Senate Foreign Relations Committee, and a regular-guy manner that played well with the blue-collar vote. He talked too much and could put his foot in his mouth, but there was no meanness about him.

Holder, a former deputy U.S. attorney general in the Clinton administration and an old Washington hand, was struck by Obama's half-open, half-inscrutable manner during the nearly eight hours of meetings they spent together going over potential veeps. Obama was diligent, bringing up small morsels of information hidden in the fat briefing books, and he acted like a law professor who calls on reluctant pupils ("I haven't heard from you," he'd say to anyone around the table who had been silent too long). A lot of politicians pretend to be inclusive; Obama actually was. But "at the end, you didn't know where he stood. When you got down to the final judgment, I had a sense, but I didn't have any kind of certainty." Holder thought Obama was being shrewd to not signal his intentions too clearly—since "people want to say what the boss wants to hear, and if they don't know, you'll get more honest advice."

At the Democratic Convention in Denver, there were no unpleasant surprises. Both Clintons gave stellar speeches that stirred the base, the true believers in the hall and millions of Democrats watching on TV. (It did not go unnoticed in Obamaland that Hillary, toward the end of the convention, reportedly assembled her closest advisers in a hotel room to discuss her prospects for 2012.) Well aware that she would be watched in some living rooms with a coldly critical eye, Michelle Obama made sure that her speech was finished a month early and memorized it. Lest there be any doubt, in the speech she distinctly declared how much she loved her country. On opening night, she was visibly nervous before the cameras, but nonetheless elegant and beautiful. Michelle and her two precocious girls engaged in some stagy but cute banter by video with Barack, who had been planted in the living room of a white middle-class family in the Midwest to watch her speech. Obama pulled his usual all-nighters to draft his

Thursday-night address. He was finally rehearsing the most important speech of his life with a teleprompter in his suite at the Hyatt when there was a knock on the door. The candidate stopped the speech to go to the door. It was room service. "All right," Obama said. "Who ordered the salad?" Axelrod sheepishly raised his finger and everyone laughed.

A few hours later, at 7:30 P.M., Obama walked slowly down a curtained hallway, dark and claustrophobic, to a small waiting area behind the stage. (The night before, Axelrod had ordered the setting toned down a little more—fewer lights, more American flags.) Obama paced in a slow circle, hand on chin, eyes downcast. He stopped, folded his arms, turned to face the stage for a few moments, then strode out, the roar of 80,000 people crashing around him.

His speech was solid, workmanlike, inspirational at moments—but not nearly as rousing as his stump speech in the primaries. Through much of the speech, Obama looked like just another Democratic presidential candidate reading from a list of promises. Obama was accepting the nomination of his party on the 45th anniversary of Martin Luther King's "I Have a Dream" speech at the Lincoln Memorial on the National Mall. Standing before the fake pillars on the Invesco Field stage, Obama briefly referred to "a young preacher from Georgia," but he did not mention King by name. Whether he was merely being poetic or avoiding using a name that still polarizes some white working-class voters, his advisers would not say.

But his closest aides were profoundly moved, perhaps less by the speech than by the distance they had come. Axelrod, who stood, crying, through the entire speech, appeared drained, all done in by the long march to this history-making night. Plouffe, the stoical campaign manager, looked nearly as wound tight as ever, but he confessed, "I cried. I was just shaking my head. You think back to all you've seen over 18, 19 months, and it's just hard to describe. Now we have nine and a half weeks to make it a reality."

Obama's chief of staff, Jim Messina, had slept only a few hours when his cell phone rang. It was still dark on the morning of Aug. 29. Messina and a few other staffers had gone to a bar to carouse after Obama's speech.

"Get your ass up," said the voice on the other end. "They picked Palin."

Messina could not mistake Plouffe's flat, no-nonsense voice, but he was still groggy. "F— you," he said. "Why are you waking me up? Stop teasing me." "I'm serious," said Plouffe. "Get up and get your team together." Messina stumbled out of bed, thinking that the Republicans must really be panicking, that they would never pick someone like Sarah Palin unless they were desperate.

Obama's plane was taking off from Denver airport around 9 A.M. when Axelrod got confirmation that McCain had indeed picked Palin as his running mate. He went to the front cabin to tell Obama and his new running mate, Joe Biden. Biden asked, "Who's Palin?"

McCain had initially wanted Joe Lieberman. The two senators were fellow romantics, deeply imbued with a sense of righteousness and honor. In mid-August, when *Newsweek*'s editor Jon Meacham was interviewing McCain aboard the campaign plane, the discussion turned to *The Winds of War*, Herman Wouk's mega-bestseller about World War II. The main character, a naval commander named Pug Henry, was a favorite of McCain's. As it turned out, Lieberman—sitting just across the aisle and listening in on the *Newsweek* interview—was a friend of Herman Wouk. "Let's go see Herman!" Lieberman piped up. "Yes!" exclaimed McCain. The two began planning a road trip out to Wouk's California home. "We can shake the money tree," McCain cackled (Wouk lives among the wealthy in Palm Springs, Calif.). McCain loved to travel with Lieberman, a fellow maverick who had stood fast on Iraq, nearly at the cost of his Senate seat in liberal Connecticut. McCain's other traveling buddy, Lindsey Graham, urged McCain to pick Lieberman, still a nominal Democrat, as a way to show that McCain put country over party label—and as a way to answer the Democrats' choice of the first African-American presidential nominee. "We've got to match history with history," Graham declared.

But when McCain brought up Lieberman's name at a secret high-level meeting held in Sedona, Ariz., to consider veep choices on Sunday, Aug. 24, his top aides balked. They warned that McCain's support among evangelicals was already soft. Lieberman was pro-choice on abortion, and a pro-choice pick would deeply antagonize the religious right, maybe even provoke a floor fight at the convention. Pollster Bill McInturff told the group that a pro-choice running mate had the potential to cause a 20-point drop in support among McCain's core voters. A small uptick in independent voters or crossover Democrats wouldn't begin to make up the difference. It would be very difficult for McCain to heal the party in the two short months before Election Day.

Lieberman was put on ice. So was former Pennsylvania governor Tom Ridge, another McCain favorite who was also pro-choice. On the shortlist, that left Tim Pawlenty, the governor of Minnesota; Mitt Romney, the former governor of Massachusetts; and a dark horse—the governor of Alaska, Sarah Palin. Romney made a certain sense; the country was heading into dark economic times and Romney, a former businessman, could compensate for McCain's self-professed lack of economic knowledge. But McCain viscerally disliked Romney during the primaries—and he owned too many houses (three, which meant that between them McCain and Romney would own 10). Pawlenty, the popular governor of a swing state the Republicans badly needed to win in November, was the safe choice. Salter especially liked Pawlenty's salt-of-the-earth qualities.

But McCain didn't want the safe choice. A top adviser would later recall that telling McCain that Pawlenty was "safe" was "like guaranteeing" that McCain would not pick him. Prodded by Schmidt and Rick Davis, McCain began asking about Palin, a first-term governor who had shaken up the Alaska political establishment by taking on her own party elders, who was fearless and defiant, who was . . . a little bit like McCain. He had called her that Sunday morning while she was attending the Alaska State Fair. It was a quick phone call, only about five minutes, and Palin had trouble hearing McCain over the noisy crowd. But McCain was intrigued. He told Salter and Schmidt to fly her down to Arizona and take a close look.

Schmidt and Salter met with her as soon as she arrived in Flagstaff on Wednesday. The three talked late into the night. Schmidt and Salter probed and pressed and looked for gaps between her views and McCain's. Palin shrugged off substantive differences. "What's the big darn deal?" she asked, smiling and, in her frontier-girl way, half defying, half flirting with her interrogators. With her flat accent and folksy charm, Palin was refreshingly down to earth, thought Salter. Salter had been wary; he had favored Pawlenty, who exuded a warm Midwestern solidity. Schmidt was pro-Palin from the beginning. He saw her potential as a conservative populist, the kind of throw-'em-red-meat, bash-the-elites politician who thrilled the Republican base that Karl Rove had so carefully nurtured through the Bush years. By picking Palin, Schmidt argued, McCain could snatch the "change" mantle away from Obama. Not for the first time, Salter came around to Schmidt's way of thinking. In the home of one of Cindy McCain's business associates, the two men tried to impress on Palin just how grueling the coming months could be. She did not seem intimidated—in the least. She was up front about her family, telling the McCain aides that her 17-year-old unmarried daughter Bristol was pregnant.

Palin stayed in Flagstaff on Wednesday night. Early on Thursday morning, Schmidt and Salter drove her to the cabin in Sedona, where she met for about an hour with McCain and chatted briefly with Cindy. Afterward, McCain and his wife took a walk along a creek running through the property. McCain consulted one last time with Schmidt and Salter. Palin would be a brave pick and she was a straight shooter, the two advisers counseled McCain. But she had no foreign-policy experience and was brand new to the national stage. McCain did not take long to decide. By 11 on that Thursday morning, he had asked Palin to join his ticket. Palin did not hesitate an instant to say yes.

The campaign was obsessively secretive about the choice. Charlie Black, one of McCain's senior advisers who was involved in the early discussions about Palin, was not told until very late Thursday night. Speechwriter Matt Scully and senior communications aide Nicolle Wallace were instructed to fly to Cincinnati and were given the name of a small, nondescript hotel. When they arrived they found Salter sitting on the curb, smoking, while Schmidt stared at his BlackBerry. The two men escorted them upstairs, saying virtually nothing. As they got out of the elevator Scully began to wonder, who the heck is behind the door? Colin Powell? Schmidt opened the door to the suite and said, "Meet our vice presidential candidate." It took Scully a few seconds to register who she was. Wallace, still a little dopey from painkillers from a root-canal operation, had no idea.

The Palin pick had the feel of a guerrilla raid, a covert operation. Salter, Schmidt and Governor Palin had checked in to the hotel under false names, pretending they were in town for a family reunion. The pirate ship was back! Muzzled and ordered to behave like a regular politician (run negative ads, avoid reporters, just read from the damn teleprompter), McCain had rebelled in his way by picking a fellow subversive—a sassy, shoot-from-the-hip, self-styled hockey mom who had shown those Big Oil boys a thing or two up in Alaska. It was romantic but also a bit impulsive. McCain's vetting operation had relied heavily on Internet searches for background checks. Davis had kept his eye on Palin for months, but it does not appear that the campaign did extensive interviewing and digging in Alaska. Some of McCain's aides were a little nervous about the Hail Mary quality of McCain's choice. As the GOP candidate introduced his running mate to the world on the morning of Friday, Aug. 29, from a university sports complex in Dayton, Ohio, one of his aides, watching from backstage, muttered, "We just threw long."

OTHER CAMPAIGN ADVISERS WERE gleeful as the pundits scrambled to make sense of it all. Some reporters did not even know how to pronounce Palin's name. But on Saturday night, a couple of reporters began asking questions about Bristol. Some had caught a glimpse of her and explained to a campaign aide that she looked, well, pregnant. The aide denied any knowledge, but Schmidt tapped one of McCain's friends, Steve Duprey, to go have an awkward conversation with Palin. Told of the reporters' nosing around, she looked out the window briefly and replied, "We have a strong family. We've been dealing with this already. We're gonna tell Bristol. We'll be fine. Let's move on. What else do you have?"

Palin remained phlegmatic the next day when the left-wing blogs began speculating that 5-month-old Trig was actually Bristol's child and that Palin was covering for her daughter. When an aide told Palin that he had started receiving calls from "respectable news organizations" demanding physiological proof that Trig was actually Palin's son, she quipped, "What, do I have to show them my stretch marks?"

At the convention in St. Paul, Palin was completely unfazed by the boys'-club fraternity she had just joined. One night, Schmidt and Salter went to her hotel room to brief her. After a minute, Palin sailed into the room wearing nothing but a towel, with another on her wet hair. She told them to chat with her laconic husband, Todd. "I'll be just a minute," she said. Salter tried to strike up a conversation. He knew that Todd was half native Alaskan and a championship snow-machine racer.

"So what's the difference between a snowmobile and a snow machine, anyway?" Salter asked. "They're the same thing," Todd replied. "Right, so why not call it a snowmobile?" Salter joshed. "Because it's a snow machine," came the reply.

Later, Schmidt and Salter went outside so that Salter could have a cigarette. "So how about the Eskimo? Is he on the level?" Schmidt asked. Salter just shrugged and took another drag.

McCain loved the whole Palin family. They seemed to offer some relief, if not a touch of anarchy, to the Straight Talk Express, which had become a bit joyless. Piper, the governor's 7-year-old, thought nothing of crawling across Joe Lieberman's lap to get to her mother. Lindsey Graham mischievously enjoyed getting the child hopped up on Mountain Dew, a beverage to which he was mildly addicted. McCain relished talking to his running mate about guns and hunting in the wild. Duprey made up a T shirt that read OUR CANDIDATE FOR VP CAN HUNT, SHOOT, DRESS, COOK HER DINNER. JOE BIDEN ORDERS TAKE-OUT. Palin put on the shirt and gave him a hug. "I *love* this shirt," she said.

The morning after his own acceptance speech, McCain was more revved up than his aides had seen him in weeks. McCain had worked hard on the speech. After wrangling with Salter, he had agreed to talk about his POW experience. Salter had privately worried that McCain might choke up, but McCain just said to Salter, "Sit where I can see you, OK?" The speech ended with a dramatic kick, as McCain implored the crowd, "Stand up, stand up, stand up and fight!" Salter leaped up in the front row, clapping and furiously gesturing for McCain to "surf the wave" of crowd response.

McCain had been too wound up to get to sleep, calling Graham at 1 A.M. ("What'd ya think, boy?" "Home run.") He was still soaring eight hours later. In Cedarburg, Wis., he gestured toward Palin and exclaimed to the crowd, "Isn't this the most marvelous running mate in the history of this nation?" McCain's crowds were usually dwarfed by his rival's rallies. But with Palin by his side, the crowds suddenly swelled to Obama-size numbers—5,000, 10,000, 15,000 people. It didn't bother McCain that the people were there to see Palin.

Patti Solis Doyle, Neera Tanden and Karen Dunn, ex-Hillary Clinton aides working for Obama, watched Palin's convention speech on the TV. They looked at each other. "This woman's trouble," said one.

The mood at the normally staid Obama headquarters had been giddy when the news of McCain's veep choice was first announced. "OK, game over," someone ventured on the morning staff phone call. But anxiety soon set in. Axelrod was offended when one staffer dared to suggest that Palin was almost as good a politician as Obama. He said he was sure that the untested rookie Alaska governor would eventually implode. Plouffe was his usual "No-Drama Obama" self, urging everyone to calm down and wait for Palin mania to pass.

One senior aide would later recall that when Obama dipped in the polls and McCain appeared to nose ahead, thanks largely to a surge of new women supporters, he wasn't so much worried about the polls as about the impact on Obama headquarters. "People went a little Kerry and Dukakis there for a couple of days," he recalled. They seemed back on their heels, unsure of how to strike back at a woman who had so gleefully mocked Obama in her convention speech.

There wasn't real panic at Obama headquarters on North Michigan Avenue—such emotionalism (normal in most campaigns) was taboo. But Palin was so unexpected a choice that some staffers were rattled. So this aide, a veteran of some nasty campaigns, would go up to staffers and say, "Get her out of your head! It's McCain!" It was an effort to force the slightly dazed staffers to see that they needed to stay focused on McCain, not his running mate.

The vast flow of information unleashed by the revolution in media technology defined issues and character at warp speed. For months, the worst rumors and conspiracy theories had been aimed at Obama: the Illinois senator had been educated in a Muslim madrassa, he had taken his oath of office on a Qur'an, he was close friends with a former Weatherman bomber from the '60s. But Obama's aides began to notice that the media and blogosphere were now buzzing with comments attributed to Palin—that she wanted to privatize Social Security, that she read the magazine of the ultrarightist John Birch Society, that she had been a member of a political party that wanted Alaska to secede from the United States. The Obama campaign did not have to do anything but watch the rumors fly. "A lot of this is being generated by people in the outside world," the Obama aide noted, adding with a smile that "I believe our rumors are, at worst, truthy," borrowing comic Stephen Colbert's definition of information that sounds true, even if it isn't. The rumor mill was starting to drag down Palin in some key places like the swing state of Florida, where she was regarded in the senior citizens' condos as a dangerous right-winger.

This aide's other metaphor for the world of TV pundits and Internet bloggers was a kids' soccer game. The swarm moved from topic to topic (and target to target) in a pack, like a herd of yelping kids chasing the ball at Saturday-morning soccer. The trick was to try to nudge the ball in a certain direction so all the kids would follow. Sometimes this was as simple as linking news stories and sending them out to Web sites. As reporters descended on Alaska to look into charges that Palin had removed the chief of Alaska's state troopers because he refused to fire Palin's ne'er-do-well ex-brother-in-law, the

Obama campaign had only to make sure the stories got wide distribution. As Palin's nomination stirred a feeding frenzy, reporters shifted their attentions from Obama to Palin. Though the Obama campaign had seeded the ground with some oppo research on Palin, with the arrival of investigative reporters like *Newsweek*'s Michael Isikoff "there's no point for us to be on it," the Obama aide noted in mid-September. Isikoff had been writing about Obama's ties to Tony Rezko. Now he was writing about Troopergate. "I thought, 'Go, Mike!'" the aide said. "Especially with the cover-up dynamic."

In mid-September, McCain was in Florida when the financial crisis broke. First the venerable investment-banking house Lehman Brothers announced it would file for bankruptcy, then the giant insurer AIG sought an emergency loan from the Federal Reserve, then the giant Merrill Lynch collapsed in a fire sale to Morgan Stanley. At a rally in Jacksonville, McCain trotted out a familiar line from his stump speech. "The fundamentals of our economy are strong," McCain insisted, as he had for months. "But these are very, very difficult times . . . I promise you, we will never put America in this position again. We will clean up Wall Street. We will reform government."

At Obama headquarters, the oppo team wasted no time. "We're grabbing up YouTube, we're driving it, everywhere," an aide recalled. "McCain says economy 'strong,'" read an e-mail from the Democratic National Committee. In Colorado, Obama openly mocked McCain, in a way that not too subtly depicted the 72-year-old senator as mentally out of it. "It's not that I think John McCain doesn't care what's going on in the lives of most Americans. I just think he doesn't know. Why else would he say, today, of all days, just a few hours ago, that the fundamentals of our economy are strong? Senator, what economy are you talking about?"

Now it was McCain's turn to seem caught unawares, to appear knocked back and unsteady. His campaign tried to explain that by "fundamentals," he meant American workers, and if Obama disagreed with that, well, then the Illinois senator was clearly against American workers. This spin was so outrageous that the regular traveling press laughed out loud.

M c CAIN, THE FIGHTER PILOT, began to swoop and veer. On the *Today* show, he declared, "We are in crisis. We are in total crisis." He called for a 9/11-style commission to investigate what exactly had gone wrong. He was ad-libbing; his staff was caught by surprise. Obama attacked again, mocking McCain for offering up "the oldest stunt in the book— you pass the buck to a commission to study a problem." McCain never mentioned the commission again.

But he continued to lurch. He announced that as president he would fire Chris Cox, the chairman of the Securities and Exchange Commission. It was pointed out to him that the president does not have the power to fire the SEC chairman, who serves a fixed term. McCain, now in forgiveness mode, called Cox a "good man" but said he would ask for his resignation anyway.

McCain's campaign slogan, "Country First," was more than a slogan to McCain. It was his life and his family's legacy. So when the crisis deepened, and Treasury Secretary Henry Paulson announced that the administration would ask Congress to pass a $700 billion bill to rescue the foundering financial institutions, McCain's instinct was to plunge in. He saw himself as Teddy Roosevelt, "the man in the arena," but he became the butt of late-night ridicule.

On the morning of Sept. 24, Barack Obama tried to call McCain to discuss a joint statement, a kind of let's-rise-above-politics declaration endorsing the bailout bill. Obama had been talking by phone to Paulson and Federal Reserve chairman Ben Bernanke. Obama's cautious instincts told him he should stay out of the negotiations between Congress and the administration. He told his aides that he did not want to say anything beyond enunciating some broad principles (the need for bipartisan oversight, for helping Main Street as well as Wall Street, for cutting off golden parachutes for executives seeking federal aid). Obama had been impressed by the sincerity—and the deep worry—of the administration's top moneymen, and he didn't want to politicize the delicate bargaining process. He contemptuously referred to George W. Bush's reign as "the incredible shrinking presidency." In his deliberate way, he wanted to try to engage his opponent in a moment of nonpartisan calming of the waters.

But McCain took his time returning Obama's phone call. McCain's aides would later say that he didn't want to talk to Obama until he had firmed up his own plans. At about 2:30 that afternoon, McCain called Obama and told him that he was thinking of suspending his campaign, asking to postpone the first debate (scheduled for two days later) and heading to Washington to join the negotiations. About five minutes after the two men hung up, McCain went public with his plans. Obama's advisers were flabbergasted. In the ever-paranoid view of rival campaigns, they thought that McCain was somehow trying to set up Obama—at first refusing his phone call, then springing on him this elaborate plan to head back to Washington and suspend the campaign. Meeting with reporters, Obama seemed slightly perplexed by McCain's to-ing and fro-ing, saying that he saw no need to put off the debate—that presidents had to be able to do two things at once, and America needed to hear from the candidates now more than ever.

Scheduled to go on David Letterman that night, McCain canceled. But instead he gave an interview to Katie Couric of CBS. The late-night comic was merciless, mocking Mc-Cain for saying that he was rushing back to Washington when he was actually over in the makeup room at CBS. Letterman portrayed McCain as a doddering fool whose Metamucil had been spiked.

McCain was in a difficult place. Like Obama, he had taken seriously the warnings that the whole financial system was in peril, and that if Congress failed to pass a rescue package by Monday, a catastrophic credit crisis loomed. At the same time, he knew from friends on Capitol Hill that House Republicans were leery of the administration's bailout plan. If he stayed aloof, and the bill failed, he knew he'd get blamed. Unlike Obama, he could not float above the fray. "Getting involved was the only move we could make," Salter later said. But McCain's romantic, take-charge streak clouded his political judgment. He may have seen himself rushing back to Washington to save the day, but Washington didn't want him—not just the Democrats, but his own Republicans brushed him off. By seeking ethics reform and a compromise on immigration in 2007, McCain had antagonized many hard-line Republican congressmen. No Republican leaders rallied to McCain when he arrived in the Capitol. "They don't like him very much," a McCain aide ruefully acknowledged. McCain called Senate Majority Leader Harry Reid to tell him his plan, and the Democratic leader coldly read from a press release accusing McCain of coming to Washington to stage a "photo op." "C'mon, Harry," McCain privately protested to Reid, whom he had known for almost three decades. (Hanging up, McCain just laughed and shook his head.) McCain had asked Bush to summon all the congressional leaders and political candidates to the White House, but the session turned into an angry farce. After the Democrats had spoken, Bush turned to John Boehner, the Republican leader in the House. Boehner told the president he couldn't muster the Republican votes necessary to pass the bill. Shouting broke out. Barney Frank, the outspoken Democrat and chairman of the House banking committee, demanded to know where McCain stood. McCain remained uncharacteristically silent. He did not want to cross his fellow Republicans. (McCain later told his aides that as the shouting began, he wondered, "What the hell is going on?" and felt as if he had wandered into a freak show.) Obama just shook his head when he reported back to his aides. He told them that Treasury Secretary Paulson had gotten down on one knee to beg House Speaker Nancy Pelosi not to blow up the deal. "Henry, I didn't know you were Catholic," she said. She told him to go beg the House Republicans.

Thrown off track, the negotiations resumed again the next day, Friday, and McCain decided he could go to the debate after all. But when he returned to Washington from the debate on Saturday and asked to be included in the negotiations, he was rebuffed. McCain worked the phones anyway, trying to muster support for the bill. When the bailout legislation went down to embarrassing defeat that Monday, McCain's inability to rally his own party was painfully obvious. Not even the four Arizona congressmen, all of whom had endorsed McCain, voted for it.

Photo by Charles Ommanney / *Newsweek*

Joe Biden and Sarah Palin greet each other at the highly-anticipated vice presidential debate.

SIX

The Great Debates

*McCain bridled at reducing his opinions to
sound bites. Obama prepped as if he were taking
the bar exam—nothing was left to chance.*

L ATER, AFTER McCAIN'S RIDE to the rescue had
been mocked in the press, some of his advisers
blamed Steve Schmidt for the fiasco. The campaign's chief strategist was forever searching for the bold
stroke, the instant game changer, but by urging McCain to
go to Washington, he had impetuously and blindly steered
the candidate into a trap. "McCain never saw it as a stunt,"
insisted one aide. But to most commentators, the bizarre
rush back to Washington seemed gimmicky—one more tac-
tical gambit in a campaign that seemed to lack any coherent
or consistent strategy.

The Obama team never took seriously McCain's announcement that he was suspending his campaign and putting off the first debate. They noted that McCain never
canceled his hotel reservations (or most of his ads) or

informed the Commission on Presidential Debates that the candidate would not be attending. Some McCain staffers later confessed they didn't think for a second he'd skip the debate. Obama's attitude toward the whole strange interlude was one of mild exasperation. When he first learned that McCain was heading for Washington, he had just silently thrown up his hands. He seemed slightly annoyed that he had to go along with the charade at the White House, which meant missing out on valuable debate-prep time, but he did not complain too loudly. There was no point; he realized soon enough that McCain had stepped on a banana peel.

Obama prepared scrupulously and relentlessly for the debates. He knew that he had delivered a mediocre to weak performance at the Saddleback forum in August. In what amounted to a preview of the formal presidential debates, the two candidates had agreed to be interviewed back to back by the Rev. Rick Warren, the bestselling evangelist, at his megachurch in California. McCain delivered short, punchy answers, and most pundits declared that he had won the day. Obama plowed along in his ponderous professor mode. Warren had asked the same questions of both candidates, and the Obama aides complained that McCain must have cheated by seeing the questions beforehand, likely furnished by aides with BlackBerrys who had watched Obama go first. McCain's advisers retorted that McCain was kept in the dark, in part because he wanted to honor the rules and also because his aides didn't want him to be distracted by trying to match Obama's answers.

Never one to wing it, Obama studied for the three official presidential debates, scheduled for roughly once a week from late September to mid-October, as if he were taking the bar exam. He memorized details on new weapons systems so he wouldn't look like a neophyte on national defense. But the real challenge, he knew, was not in the details of policy or his mastery of defense-spending arcana. He would need to show something more ineffable but profound—a true command presence. As his aides never ceased to remind him, he would have to look "presidential."

The topic of the first debate was meant to be foreign policy, McCain's strong suit. Obama did not object. Better to get it out of the way—to deal with his perceived weakness right away, to outperform expectations. Inevitably, given the crisis in Washington, the first questions from the moderator, Jim Lehrer of PBS, were bound to focus on the proposed bailout and the economy. But that was all right, too. Obama's burden was to show that he was ready to step up to crisis, that he would not be learning on the job in the Oval Office.

In debate prep, Obama's advisers repeatedly instructed him: Do not get personal. Stay calm and in control. Stay presidential. The voters know you represent change; now you've got to persuade them to see you as president.

"Command and control: we told him, 'Write it down on your pad when you go in,'" said Joel Benenson, a pollster who was on the debate-prep team. The candidates were not allowed to bring notes in with them, but they could take notes once they got onstage. Benenson later told a *Newsweek* reporter that he doubted that Obama took their advice to write it down. The candidate didn't need to: "He knew that was the mission," said Benenson.

Obama was up against McCain's strength and experience in the national-security realm, but he was also confronting a deeper stereotype, a curse that had kept the Democrats out of the White House for 20 of the last 28 years. Ever since the days of Jimmy Carter, a majority of Americans had consistently told pollsters that they trusted the Republicans more on the issue of security—not just abroad, but at home. To use ancient and more or less discredited (but still potent) clichés, the Democrats were the Mommy party, comforting the needy and weak, while the Republicans were the Daddy party, keeping the family safe from threats. In the debates, it was critical that Obama come across looking like Dad. His hope was that McCain would appear to be the crotchety uncle who lived up in the attic.

At Obama's debate rehearsals, held repeatedly through the late summer and with increasing frequency and intensity in September, the role of McCain was played by Gregory Craig—the ace Washington lawyer dubbed as one of "the Kool-Aid boys" by a bemused Obama back in 2006. After urging Obama to run, Craig had become an informal foreign-policy adviser to him. A trial lawyer, Craig was agile and could, if necessary, come on strong. The expectation was that McCain would condescend to Obama as a wet-behind-the-ears rookie, so Craig played his role accordingly. "Do not lecture me about the war," Craig-as-McCain said, glowering at Obama, in debate prep. "Do not tell me how to deploy men in combat. I was flying a jet over Vietnam when you were in grade school."

Obama was tutored to seem stern and unflinching, to treat McCain respectfully but to stand up to him. He rehearsed a moment when he could turn to McCain and counterattack—to begin by saying, "You were wrong about Iraq . . ." and work through a litany of McCain's misjudgments. The Obama team was sure that McCain would criticize him for having said, in a Democratic debate in the summer of 2007, that he would be willing to meet with Iran's Mahmoud Ahmadinejad and Cuba's Fidel Castro. Obama was instructed to point out that McCain was so averse to personal diplomacy that he had declined to meet with the president of Spain. Obama can be a little bloodless and dull in his preternatural calm, but his goofy side showed up at debate prep. He would appear very somber and emphatic when he accosted Craig/McCain for refusing to speak to the president of Spain. "You wouldn't even talk to the president of Spain!" he would intone with mock gravity. Then he would begin to giggle. He was told that he should attack McCain for saying that it was enough to "muddle through" on Afghanistan. "Muddle through!" Obama would exclaim and dissolve into giggles. It was as if he refused to take the theater of mock indignation too seriously.

Obama never lost his ironic detachment, even when he was preparing for the most important public appearances of his life. A little comic relief was called for. In the carefully prepared world of Obamaland, nothing was left to chance. The rehearsal room in Clearwater, Fla., was an exact replica of the debate stage where Obama met McCain in the first debate at Ole Miss. No detail was overlooked. The podiums were set at the precise angles. Obama rehearsed in the evenings, to match his natural circadian rhythms. For the second debate, a town-hall format, Obama was told to be careful to hold the mike by his side—not straight up in his lap—when he sat down. The same instructions had been given to John Kerry four years ago. It wasn't hard to persuade the candidates to mind the advice, said an aide; all you had to do was show them a video.

Obama's debate coach, Michael Sheehan, a veteran of many campaign psychodramas over the years, was struck by the senator's calmness. The candidate was always in control of his feelings. During one afternoon prep session, Obama begged off. "I'm a little tired and a little cranky," he told a roomful of aides. "I'm going to my room for a half hour and I'll be in better shape to work with." He reappeared 30 minutes later, ready for work. Obama was, as ever, self-possessed—his own best judge of his mood and strength. After a full-dress mock debate in the evening, when it was time to review the tape of his performance, Obama turned to Sheehan and said, "Michael, I'm tired." He was not complaining, Sheehan recalled; he was just being matter-of-fact. Nothing seemed to rattle Obama. He had a way of retreating into his own little world. During one of the debate preps, the lights blew, flickering on and off like a strobe light from the 1970s disco craze. Obama stood behind the podium, quietly singing the song "Disco Inferno," last popular in the heyday of *Saturday Night Fever*.

On the day of the first debate, in Jackson, Miss., Obama ate a late lunch with Valerie Jarrett, Eric Whitaker and Marty Nesbitt, his closest Chicago pals. He was serenely calm, Jarrett recalled. He talked about having done everything he'd set out to do; he said he had no regrets. Later, on-stage, Obama often politely agreed with McCain (11 times), but he did not let himself be bullied. McCain called his opponent's ideas "naive" and "dangerous," but Obama, smiling impassively, did not take the bait. There were no knockdown blows or surprising moments. The drama was more in the nature of a highly stylized Kabuki theater—a kind of playing out of a hoary ritual that was more timeless than topical, more deferential to political tropes (Always praise the goodness of the American people! Do not require them to sacrifice!) than it was responsive to the challenges ahead. In some ways, the candidates seemed oddly irrelevant to the fiscal crisis. Asked if they supported the bailout bill hanging fire, or unresolved, in Congress, they both gave tepid endorsements and dodged around the question of whether their campaign promises needed to be tempered in any way.

Political reporters, who tend to score debates as prize fights, were disappointed. Some decreed that McCain had landed the most punches, racked up the most points. But in the public polls that followed the debate, Obama emerged as the consensus winner. He had been the cool and steady one. McCain had seemed at first quite subdued, then a little cranky and peevish at moments. He would not look at

Obama despite Lehrer's admonition to the candidates to directly talk to each other. The overall effect was a role reversal, a flip-flop of predebate expectations: the candidate who looked most "presidential" was Obama.

AFTER THE FIRST DEBATE, McCAIN and his handlers reviewed the videotape. Why, one aide asked him, did you never look at Obama? Because you told me not to! McCain retorted. It was true. McCain's debate coach, Brett O'Donnell, had noted Obama's tendency to look directly at an opponent while attacking, and he had instructed McCain not to get sucked in by meeting his gaze. But McCain had taken the advice a little too literally. "We didn't tell you not to look at him *at all*," one aide chided him. (Advisers also told McCain to soften his blows by saying "what my opponent doesn't understand"—another trope he overused.) The veteran of a thousand morning talk shows, McCain was accustomed to speaking directly to the camera, not to his inquisitor in the studio. But in this case his experience was a liability.

McCain had looked forward to prepping for debates about as much as he did to studying for exams in school. The preparations for the rehearsals were "a mess," recalled one of his top advisers. The candidate at first resisted debate prep, then couldn't get enough of it. McCain didn't settle on Congressman Rob Portman to play the role of Obama until three weeks before the first debate. (Craig had been preparing for his McCain turn for months.) When the rehearsals finally began, McCain worked hard, and he sought feedback on his answers, but the plethora of opinions was not always helpful. Pretty much anyone was allowed to sit in—all the top campaign aides, as well as, it seemed to one exasperated adviser, "random senators." As he prepared for the second debate, there were "too many voices," this adviser later lamented. "It was getting him tied up." McCain would listen to different people telling him that he had to say something in a certain way, and then he would go onstage "thinking in his mind: OK, I have to get 15 things in. What are the 15 things?" recalled the adviser—"rather than just being himself. His personality never came through." Accustomed to detailed debate in the Senate, he bridled at reducing his opinions to sound bites. The off-the-cuff charmer and disarmer from the old Straight Talk Express was missing from the second debate, a town-hall format that was supposed to be the most comfortable setting for McCain.

Various advisers cautioned McCain against being too aggressive. They recalled that he had been particularly caustic, almost brutal, toward Mitt Romney during the primary debates in January. McCain tried to joke that he was just getting it out of his system, but Mark Salter interjected, "C'mon, John, that was like shooting the wounded."

McCain's coaches worried about the candidate's undisguised disdain for Obama. McCain dismissed his opponent as grandiose. He found Obama to be affected; he was irked by footage of Obama swaggering along, dangling his coat coolly over his shoulder. For the battered McCain, whose arms were so stiff that he could not raise them to comb his own hair, Obama's smooth-operator style was pretentious.

Tension grew as McCain prepared for the second debate, the town-hall format in Nashville on Oct. 7. Pygmalion-like, Salter kept trying to craft the John McCain of their heroic books—plain-spoken yet eloquent, quietly noble in his humble greatness. Salter was "tightly wound," observed an aide who was present at the debate preps. "He was really pressing John to say things exactly like he would say them." On a Saturday session in a dingy conference room at the Radisson Hotel in Phoenix, McCain seemed distracted, off his game. He maintained his sense of humor. "Duprey!" he would periodically yell to friend Steve Duprey, who sat in the back reading a book or a newspaper. "Why haven't you fallen asleep yet?" But at one point McCain flubbed an answer to the faux moderator (played by Charlie Black, who was so serious about his role that he wouldn't let McCain or Portman go to the bathroom during precisely timed rehearsals). Everyone in the room, including McCain, knew that the answer had been off base. Salter stood up and said, "Every part of that answer was completely wrong." McCain collapsed into his chair, deflated. "Well, let's give up," he said, exasperated. He wanted to go to his cabin in Sedona. The next day a smaller group held a more focused practice session there, under the Arizona sun. McCain's sense of humor recovered, and he began teasing staffers. "Should I really feed you people after that?" he cracked as they broke for dinner.

To ease the mood before the first debate, McCain's advisers had shown the candidate a YouTube video of Joe Biden awkwardly encouraging a supporter at a rally to stand up—not realizing the man was in a wheelchair. McCain was amused by Biden's amiable talkiness. He was relieved to face him as the veep choice and not Hillary Clinton, whom the McCain camp had truly feared. At the vice presidential debate on Oct. 2, McCain was delighted to see that Sarah Palin had irritated Biden. Watching the TV with some aides, McCain exclaimed, "He looks like an angry old senator!" The staffers were awkwardly silent, unsure if McCain appreciated the irony of his statement and hoping that he would experience a flash of self-recognition in time for his own performance in debate No. 2, just five days away.

He APPARENTLY DID NOT. Haltingly pacing the stage, his limbs stiff from old wounds, McCain repeated the expression "my friends" until it was a meaningless punctuation mark. Obama stayed perched on his stool, watching, and not saying anything very memorable or that might in some way impede his steady march upward in the polls. McCain's aides later grumbled to a *Newsweek* reporter that the town-hall format was a joke, that moderator Tom Brokaw asked too many questions and that the candidates couldn't really engage the voters with two-minute answers. But all of that may have been irrelevant. The afternoon of the second debate, the Dow plunged 500 points. As the economy sank, the fortunes of Obama—as the Democratic candidate after eight years of Republican rule—inevitably rose. McCain could have performed flawlessly and still succumbed to economic reality.

After the town-hall debate, Salter and Schmidt reunited with a dozen or so members of the traveling press corps at a karaoke bar in Nashville. It had been months since the duo had had a night out with reporters. Salter, who had sung in a band in college, was cajoled into singing a few tunes. Before long, and after a drink or two, he was into it. Under pressure from the reporters, Schmidt joined him for a chorus of Johnny Cash's "Folsom Prison Blues." Schmidt even sang "Rocky Mountain High," to squeals from the increasingly inebriated reporters. But then he went off and sat quietly. Schmidt looked worn out, his burly body weighed by stress and the woes of the campaign, his relentless stare dimmed by exhaustion. He ignored political questions and talked quietly about his family. Salter, on the other hand, had found his groove. Standing in the middle of the bar, dressed in his ubiquitous corduroy jacket, he bellowed "More Dylan!" until he had belted out every Bob Dylan song the bar had. Reporters sang loud, drunken backup and tried to get Salter to join them in boy-band dance moves. It was the first time anyone had seen Salter look as if he was having fun in a long time.

Salter had long deferred to Schmidt. McCain's speech and book-writing amanuensis was more than a decade and a half older than the campaign's chief strategist, but Schmidt was a take-charge type, while Salter preferred to play the observer and *consigliere*. The two men kept each other laughing with deadpan, self-deprecating humor. Salter joked about Schmidt's mathematical limitations, noting that his friend was so dyslexic he could barely read a poll. But as a story-teller, Salter admired Schmidt's ability to lay out a narrative, the storyline that every campaign needs to make its candidate more appealing (or less unappealing) to voters. Schmidt had been instrumental in launching the "No Surrender Tour" after the campaign staggered through the summer of 2007, and in July he had revived the flagging campaign again with the "celebrity" ad. Salter had fully come around to Schmidt's skeptical view of the press. Once, after Salter refused to let a couple of snarky bloggers aboard the Straight Talk Express, Schmidt called him with congratulations for staying firm. The two advisers had finally managed to persuade McCain to stop reading the political coverage of *The New York Times* after he had been irked by a couple of critical stories in late September.

Salter never criticized Schmidt, either to other reporters or within the campaign. He wanted to honor McCain's admonition against backbiting by his top advisers, and the two remained close friends. With a *Newsweek* reporter, Schmidt rebuffed media gossip that he had grown apart from Salter. But he spent less time kicking back with him, in part because Schmidt was more often in headquarters than on the road. One evening at the bar, when Schmidt came over and a gaggle of reporters quickly turned their attention away from Salter (who was a familiar presence) and to Schmidt (who was not), Salter cracked that "Schmidt never joins a conversation. He commandeers it."

Though he denied it to *Newsweek*, Salter seemed troubled by the campaign's relentlessly negative tone. The Obama campaign was not exactly running on sweetness and light—at least a third of Obama's ads attacked McCain. The Obama campaign did not hesitate to imply, through its choice of language, that McCain's "erratic" actions might have something to do with his advanced age. Obama's admen used the shameless old Democratic trick of trying to scare elderly voters by suggesting, based on little evidence, that McCain planned to cut their Social Security benefits in half. But by early October, virtually all of McCain's ads were negative. The press was increasingly painting him as a bitter old man. This seemed to pain Salter, who had worked so hard to craft a heroic, selfless image of John McCain—the idealization that McCain himself had wanted to live up to, but now seemed to be putting at risk by traveling the low road.

Salter was particularly aggrieved by a McCain ad suggesting that Obama wanted sex education taught to preschoolers. He predicted, correctly, that *The New York Times* would jump all over the ad and lambaste McCain. But no one on the senior team seemed to care what *The New York Times* wrote anymore. Schmidt wanted to kick the Gray Lady off the campaign plane for good. Though polling suggested that such a move would play well with the GOP base, Salter vehemently protested that it would be foolish to cut off the *Times*, and Schmidt backed off.

ONE OF MCCAIN'S ADVISERS SAID of Salter, "We call him McCain's wife." As one senior adviser explained it, "I've done a lot of campaigns . . . and the candidate's wife is always a bit of a problem. The candidate's wife, her job is different from everyone else's. Our job is for Candidate X to win. The candidate's wife's job is always to protect the candidate. Those two goals are often in conflict." A *Newsweek* reporter asked the strategist if Salter was just reflecting Mc-Cain's preferences. "If that were a true husband and wife, how would you know?" the adviser answered. As for Mc-Cain's actual wife, "she has not been one bit of a problem. I'm a big Cindy fan."

In mid-October, one senior adviser noted to the *Newsweek* reporter, "Of late there has been more separation between [Salter] and Steve [Schmidt] because, I think, he thinks we are taking McCain down a path that we shouldn't. And quite frankly, we are. It's the difference between scorched earth and having as little collateral damage as possible."

The Palin media rollout was a particularly destructive weapon. Vice presidential candidates often act as attackers, allowing their running mates to float above the fray. But Palin's exuberant assaults on Obama ended up dragging McCain into the middle of the fight, where he seemed decidedly uncomfortable.

Palin was being handled by Nicolle Wallace, a veteran of the hardball politics of the Bush-Cheney campaign (she had been a press-bashing director of communications). Recruited by Schmidt, Wallace had come from a stint as a commentator at CBS. She had the disastrous idea of making Palin available only for a series of high-profile media interviews, and then over-prepared her with a cram course of talking points. It was embarrassing to watch Palin grope for answers to Katie Couric's questions—and thanks to YouTube, more than 10 million voters witnessed it. "She is not a dumb person," said a senior McCain adviser. "She is an intelligent person, but we made her so uptight." Some old McCain hands on the campaign were sharply critical of the Bush-Cheney alumni brought onboard by Schmidt. Wallace and the others had not only botched the handling of Palin, in the view of the old McCainiacs; they didn't understand that McCain needed to be McCain. (Wallace took responsibility, in an edgy kind of way: "I keep trying to get someone to write that it's my stupid strategy," she told a *Newsweek* reporter. "I should be fired. I've offered my resignation twice in the spirit of Dwight D. Eisenhower, taking responsibility, and no one will take it." In truth, Wallace was in a tough place: Palin was no longer taking much coaching from her. Feeling that she had been overmanaged for her one-on-one debut with a network anchor—Charlie Gibson of ABC—Palin had rebuffed Wallace's help with her Couric interview.)

Palin skillfully handled her debate with Joe Biden by essentially ignoring the questions posed by the "media elite" (PBS's Gwen Ifill, the moderator). And she was rousing at rallies of true believers. "God bless America, you guys get it!" she enthused a few minutes after 9 on a muggy October morning in Clearwater, Fla. An enormous American flag was suspended on a crane over her head. "Drill, baby, drill!" screamed the virtually all-white crowd of several thousand. She started in on Obama. "I am just so fearful that this is not a man who sees America the way you and I see America," she said.

She brought up William Ayers, the former Weather Underground bomber who was acquainted with Obama through Chicago politics. "I'm afraid that this is someone who sees America as imperfect enough to work with a former domestic terrorist who targeted his own people."

In tailored jackets and skirts, she was glamorous and tastefully sexy (Politico reported that the McCain campaign spent $150,000 to dress her and her family). She was speaking before a working-class crowd in Bethlehem, Pa., a few days later when a man in the audience shouted out, "You're a hottie!" Onstage, John McCain laughed, and Cindy laughed louder. Not missing a beat, Palin flashed a killer smile and asked, "Now, what does that have to do with anything?"

But in other ways she was a little too hot. At the Clearwater rally, someone in the crowd used a racial epithet about a black sound man for NBC, and someone else reportedly yelled "Kill him!" in an ambiguous reference to either Ayers or Obama. By the end of the week, YouTube was showing film clips of Palin crowds shouting "Treason!", "Off with his head!" and "He is a bomb!" At a McCain-Palin rally in Strongsville, Ohio, a man called Obama a "one-man terror cell," and in one unsettling film clip a voter's young daughter exclaims about Obama, "You need gloves to touch him!"

Palin, the polls showed, had succeeded in rallying the Republican base. But she, or the simmering anger around her, helped make Obama supporters out of countless independent voters.

On the weekend between the second and third debates, Congressman John Lewis—a civil-rights hero who had been beaten while staging nonviolent protests during the 1960s—issued a press release accusing McCain and Palin of "playing with fire" and seeming to compare McCain to former Alabama governor George Wallace, a segregationist infamous for stirring racial fears. McCain was stunned. He had devoted a chapter to Lewis in one of his books, *Why Courage Matters*. He so admired Lewis that he had taken his children to meet him.

MCCAIN WAS ON HIS BUS, ABOUT to board a plane in Moline, Ill., when he read the remarks on an aide's BlackBerry. He was so dumbfounded that he held the plane on the tarmac while he considered how to respond. Salter, who had penned the chapter on Lewis, urged McCain to remain more dignified than Lewis had been in his remarks. But Schmidt called in from headquarters brimming with outrage. "Sir," said Schmidt, "he called you a racist. It must be responded to." Nicolle Wallace agreed. Salter was not so sure. He was "very pained" over the incident, Schmidt later recalled about Salter, but his instinct told him not to get his boss into a name-calling fight with a martyr of the civil-rights movement. McCain decided to go with Schmidt and put out a strong statement calling on Obama to "immediately and personally repudiate these outrageous and divisive comments." (Obama left it to a spokesman to blandly state, "Senator Obama does not believe that John McCain or his policy criticism is in any way comparable to George Wallace or his segregationist policies.")

According to several aides, McCain had trouble shaking his sadness over Lewis's statement. To the reporters traveling with McCain, the candidate seemed uncertain, as if he was not quite sure what he had gotten himself into. In an effort to raise doubts about Obama, McCain had given a stump speech in which he asked the audience, "Who *is* Barack Obama?" At an earlier rally in Albuquerque a man shouted, "A terrorist!" McCain paused, taken aback. He looked surprised, troubled. But he continued with the speech. (Salter later said McCain wasn't sure that he had heard correctly.)

A couple of days later, at a rally in Lakeville, Minn., he seemed to find his bearings. "If you want a fight, we will fight," he said. "But we will be respectful. I admire Senator Obama and his accomplishments. I will respect him, and I want—no, no," McCain said to loud boos. "I want everyone to be respectful." In the question-and-answer period, a middle-aged woman in a bright red shirt took the mike and said, "I can't trust Obama. I have read about him, and he's not, he's not, he's a, um—he's an Arab."

"No. No, ma'am. No, ma'am. No, ma'am. No, ma'am," McCain said, taking back the wireless mike. "He's a decent family man, a citizen, that I just happen to have disagreements with on fundamental issues; that's what this campaign is about. He's not. Thank you."

On Oct. 12, the Sunday night before the last debate, McCain's core group of advisers—Steve Schmidt, Rick Davis, adman Fred Davis, strategist Greg Strimple, pollster Bill McInturff and strategy director Sarah Simmons—met to review the state of the campaign. The polling numbers were grim. The question on the table was whether it was time to call on McCain and tell him it was over, that he no longer had a chance to win. The consensus in the room was no, not yet, not while he still had a "pulse." The pulse was faint, one of the strategists said afterward, and getting fainter—McCain had no better than a 10 or 15 percent shot at the presidency. The group knew he would have to have a very strong last debate to improve the odds even a little.

There was grumbling that Palin had jumped the gun by bringing up Ayers at her rallies before the campaign could properly do the groundwork with a rollout strategy and ads. (At one rally, she had talked about Obama "palling around with terrorists.") Palin was mad at her handlers. Reportedly, she felt that Wallace and Schmidt had poorly coached and advised her. One adviser later speculated that she impulsively talked about Ayers because she felt thwarted—she had really wanted to bring up the Rev. Jeremiah Wright. (Actually, Palin was feeling hurt and angry over the tabloid treatment of her 17-year-old daughter Bristol, and decided—on her own—that Ayers should be fair game. McCain's advisers were working on a strategy that would launch an Ayers attack the following week, but McCain had not signed off on it, and Salter was resisting.)

The campaign's internal polls showed that those lower-income swing voters in industrial states had not forgotten about Wright. In the view of some of his advisers, McCain had a chance to really hurt Obama by dredging up those videotapes of his long-time pastor crying "Goddam America!" But McCain did not want to. He did not want to do anything that smacked of racism. Some of his aides had quietly wished that the 527s, the independent-expenditure groups, would do the campaign's dirty work by running ads about Wright. Yet others worried that the 527s would indeed run lurid ads about Wright—and that McCain would get the blame. In any case, the big conservative moneymen who might fund such a smear campaign were lying low, and not just because their portfolios were suffering in the stock-market dive. They didn't want to be called racist, either.

McCain had set firm boundaries: no Jeremiah Wright; no attacking Michelle Obama; no attacking Obama for not serving in the military. McCain balked at an ad using images of children that suggested that Obama might not protect them from terrorism; Schmidt vetoed ads suggesting that Obama was soft on crime (no Willie Hortons); and before word even got to McCain, Schmidt and Salter scuttled a "celebrity" ad of Obama dancing with talk-show host Ellen DeGeneres (the sight of a black man dancing with a lesbian was deemed too provocative).

In mid-October, Cindy McCain surprised reporters by tak-ing the stage and saying that, as the mother of a Marine in Iraq, she felt "a cold chill" after Obama's vote in the Senate to cut off funds for the troops (a charge that was not accu-rate). It was rare for the candidate's wife to thrust herself into the spotlight. In late September, she had abruptly dropped off the campaign plane and returned to Arizona. A *Newsweek* reporter spotted her at a hotel in Ohio; she looked upset. A staffer told the reporter that McCain and his wife had been fighting over his assent to an interview in *The New Yorker* magazine. Cindy had been hoping he would refuse it as punishment for a long, unflattering profile of her that had appeared in print. It was the last straw for Cindy, who found the campaign trail emotionally and physically trying. She in-sisted that an aide install an extra curtain around McCain's and her seats on the plane to grant them additional privacy. Anxious that Cindy's stress was affecting McCain, one staffer, who usually appreciates her lighthearted company, privately expressed some relief that she had dropped off for a short while.

"I'm worried," Gregory Craig said to a *Newsweek* reporter in mid-October. He was concerned that the frenzied atmosphere at the Palin rallies would encourage someone to do something violent toward Obama. He was not the only one in the Obama campaign thinking the unthinkable. The campaign was provided with reports from the Secret Service showing a sharp and very disturbing increase in threats to Obama in September and early October. Michelle was shaken by the vituperative crowds and the hot rhetoric from the GOP candidates. "Why would they try to make people hate us?" she asked Valerie Jarrett. Several of Obama's friends in the Senate were shocked by the GOP rabble-rousing. Dick Durbin, the U.S. senator from Illinois who pushed for early Secret Service coverage for Obama, called Lindsey Graham, who was traveling with McCain. (Graham scoffed at the call as "an orchestrated attempt to push a narrative" about McCain going negative. He said he told Durbin, "OK, buddy, but remember—that goes both ways.")

For the first two debates, the Obama campaign asked members of focus groups to turn dials to measure their response to the candidates. Every time Obama seemed to quarrel with McCain, or even criticize him, his readings went down. For the third debate, the word went out: no *Crossfire*-type wrangling. The Obama campaign had been bracing for attacks on his relationship to Bill Ayers for months (in the spring, focus groups had been assembled to gauge how those attacks would play to the public). The format of the third debate brought the two candidates almost side by side, seated at a table, so Obama would have a more difficult time keeping his distance. But he prepared, as always, to keep his cool. In rehearsal, Craig-as-McCain was so over the top in his efforts to bait Obama that both men dissolved into giggles at one point. But at other times, Obama allowed himself to get angry. Later, when he watched a video of the rehearsal, he saw himself and vowed: no shouting, no talking over McCain. A little subtle needling might be permissible. The goal, said debate-prep coach Michael Sheehan, was to make McCain look like Mr. Wilson, the cranky next-door neighbor in the comic strip *Dennis the Menace*, always yelling at the neighborhood kids.

At first, Joe the Plumber made the Obamaites anxious. When McCain brought him up at the third debate, suggesting that Obama wanted to raise his taxes and "spread the wealth around," Obama operatives worried that the candidate had been somehow set up—that Joe, who had chatted briefly with Obama at a rally, had been sent there to entrap the candidate before the cameras (a clip had already shown up on YouTube). A quick run of computer databases suggested that if Joe was a plant, he was a poor one. He was not a licensed plumber, he had some messy court papers dealing with his family life, his name wasn't Joe (his real name was Samuel Wurzelbacher) and it was unlikely that Obama's plan would actually raise his taxes.

As usual with the McCain campaign, Joe the Plumber had more to do with impulse than planning. As Lindsey Graham told the story, he had been awakened at 4:30 on the morning of the final debate. It was McCain on the phone. "I can't sleep," said the candidate. "Well, now neither can I," said a sleepy Graham. He stumbled on down to McCain's hotel room. McCain was vibrating with nervous energy, rehearsing his lines on his least favorite subject, the economy. He was racing through a section on taxes, not really paying attention to the words, and said, "Obama will raise taxes, raise taxes on ordinary folks like Joe the Plumber." Graham perked up, as did Cindy, who was sitting there patiently with her agitated husband. "John, what was that you just said?" Cindy asked. "About the plumber?" Lindsey added. The three spent the rest of the session talking about how to work him into the debate.

Joe the Plumber and McCain's nervous energy failed to deliver the knockout blow required for the final debate. With still almost three weeks to go until Election Day, to the Obamaites the biggest threat now seemed to be overconfidence. On one of the cable shows, Bob Shrum, who had run the 2004 John Kerry campaign, had already declared that Obama was going to be the next president of the United States. A reporter sent an e-mail to Obama adman Jim Margolis informing him of Shrum's prediction, along with a reminder that Shrum was also the guy who—shortly after the first exit polls wrongly predicted a Kerry victory on Election Day 2004—had said to Senator Kerry, "May I be the first to call you Mr. President." Margolis quickly wrote back, "Oh, my God, we're doomed."

Axelrod's gloomy nature was working overtime, imagining scenarios that would bring the whole triumphant processional to a nightmare ending. He understood that late-deciding voters tended to be less informed (and thus susceptible to smears and rumors) and more conservative. Axelrod worried that the race would tighten in the late going as these voters came off the fence. His fear was that Obama's comfortable lead would dwindle to a few points. Axelrod had always dismissed race as a nonissue in the campaign and chastised news organizations (especially *Newsweek*) for writing about it. But the more he scoffed at talk of race, the more it clearly gnawed at him. He had come up in the cauldron of racial politics in Chicago and prided himself in his ability to make Obama appealing to white voters. But on some level, he couldn't quite believe it would work out.

On a conference call with his staff after the third debate, Obama warned against overconfidence. He reminded staffers that the campaign had been sure of success once before, only to see victory slip away. His words were later posted in the bathroom at the headquarters on North Michigan Avenue: FOR THOSE OF YOU WHO ARE FEELING GIDDY OR COCKY OR THINK THIS IS ALL SET, I HAVE JUST TWO WORDS FOR YOU: NEW HAMPSHIRE.

Obama at a campaign rally in Denver, Colorado, on October 26, 2008.

(Photo by Charles Ommanney / *Newsweek*)

SEVEN

The Final Days

*Obama was leading in the polls, even in
red states like Virginia. But McCain almost
seemed to glory in being the underdog.*

THE OBAMA CAMPAIGN RAN THE biggest, best-financed get-out-the-vote campaign in the history of American politics. It wanted to turn out minorities and the young, groups that traditionally stay away from the polls. For the cautious, self-consciously virtuous Obamaites, this worthy goal posed some special challenges.

The campaign wanted to reach out to young black men, but in a way that would not antagonize white voters. The rap artist Jay-Z offered to perform in concert for Obama in October, but the campaign was "nervous," recalled Jim Messina, the campaign chief of staff. Black leaders from the community in Detroit and Miami pleaded with Obama headquarters, Messina recalled, saying, in effect, "You keep saying to us, 'Go produce sporadic African-American young voters.' Give us the tools. Jay-Z is a tool and you have to give him to us."

Warily, the campaign agreed but still called the rap star's management to ask him not to say anything about McCain or Palin onstage, for fear that the rapper would make crude or incendiary remarks that would wind up on *Fox News*. Jay-Z agreed not to riff on the Republican candidates, but he said he wanted to perform a song, "Blue Magic," that includes the line "Push, money over broads, f– Bush/Chef, guess what I cooked? Made a lot of bread and kept it off the books."

At a concert on Oct. 5 in Miami, Jay-Z decided to skip the line about Bush, but the crowd, familiar with the words, roared it out anyway, as giant portraits of Bush and Obama lit up the backdrop. The incident passed largely unnoticed by the media—and the Obama campaign registered 10,000 new voters in Miami.

"Walking-around money" is an old and somewhat disreputable political practice of dispensing cash to local pols, grassroots community leaders and preachers to get out the vote on Election Day, particularly in poorer areas inhabited by racial and ethnic minorities. As money changes hands, a certain amount of winking is typically involved; not all of the funds go to, say, hiring drivers or passing out leaflets, and the recipients are not shy about asking. (During the Robert F. Kennedy campaign for president in 1968, Kennedy operatives made sure not to bid up the going rate for walking-around money, or to hand it out too early, lest they have to pay twice.)

On Oct. 21, Michael Strautmanis was riding, along with a *Newsweek* reporter, through the streets of Philadelphia in an aged Honda Accord driven by a baby-faced law grad who had volunteered for the campaign 10 days earlier. Strautmanis had been a close friend of Michelle and Barack Obama since he worked at the same Chicago law firm in the late '80s. He was on his way—or so he thought—to a one-on-one meeting with a local Democratic congressman. But word arrived that the meeting had been expanded to include the Democratic city committee, a local power center in Philadelphia's Democratic politics. One of the city committee's roles was as collector and dispenser of walking-around money. Obama had refused on principle to hand out walking-around money during the Pennsylvania primary, which he lost by eight points.

"I'm not doing that," Strautmanis said, to no one in particular. He quickly called a friend to arrange a place where he could meet with the congressman—alone. Next was a meeting with a state senator, who greeted Strautmanis like an old friend, even though they had never met. The state senator said he was in awe of Obama. "He's the greatest bulls–ter in the world!" the politician exclaimed. "I know he's bulls–ting me, but it feels good!" Sensing he was perhaps being a little too frank, the state senator said, "I want to be as helpful as I can." Strautmanis said the campaign planned to "overwhelm the system" with a massive turnout. They planned to have volunteers knock on every door of every likely voter in Philadelphia, three times—on Saturday, Monday and Election Day. The trick then was to get them to the polls. The state senator suggested buses "with AC and a healthcare worker onboard" for senior citizens. "And street money," the senator said. "I know you guys didn't do it in the primary, but . . . "

Strautmanis continued, asking, "What about the churches?" The senator became a little vague, or perhaps coy. "The churches are . . ." he began, pausing. "They're in a different place." He suggested some churches might hold out support if they're not courted, but, the senator added, "After he gets elected they'll be the first ones asking, 'Can we get to the ball?'" Strautmanis politely changed the subject. "So what are you working on, policywise?" he asked.

After the meeting, Strautmanis admitted to seeing some benefit. "I think we should do it," the Obama aide told a *Newsweek* reporter. "It's just part of the culture here, and what will it cost? A couple of hundred grand? . . . For a lot of people, if they don't get it, they just flat-out won't engage." (The Obama campaign ultimately refused to provide any walking-around money, though as Politico reported, some was provided by local sources.)

In some ways, the technological challenges were less complicated for the young vote getters of Team Obama. On Election Day, campaigns need to find a way to turn out supporters who have not yet voted. This means matching lists of supporters with lists of voters appearing at the polls. During the primaries, the Obama campaign was able to update its lists every three hours, a pretty impressive frequency.

B<small>UT NOT GOOD ENOUGH</small>. The geeks at New Media, working with the field department, had created a program that would allow a "flusher"—the term for a volunteer who goes out to round up nonvoters on Election Day—to know exactly who had, and had not, voted in real time. The New Media magicians dubbed it Project Houdini, because of the way names disappear off the list instantly once people are identified as they wait in line at their local polling station. "I have no idea how [Project Houdini] will work," Steve Schale, the campaign's Florida state director, told *Newsweek* a week before Election Day. "But if it does work, it will redefine get-out-the-vote. . . . It's an amazing, fascinating tool, and if it works, it will be the model that everyone uses going forward."

In past presidential campaigns, Democrats relied on loose organizations of volunteers and labor unions to get out the vote. This time around, the Obama campaign was as tightly run as the old Karl Rove Republican machine. In the battleground state of Ohio, "instead of volunteers assembling at 200 parking lots at union halls, we have 1,400 neighborhood teams in the state that we have spent six months recruiting and training and managing," said Jon Carson, the overseer of Obama's national network of volunteers. "We've taken the best of those volunteers, and they're giving us 40, 50, 60 hours a week. They're empowered, and we made them accountable. I can tell from here in Chicago; did you make the phone calls, the door knocks?"

With five days to go, the campaign's chief strategist, David Axelrod, looked less anxious than usual. Indeed, he almost seemed well rested. Speaking with a *Newsweek* reporter at an Obama rally in Sarasota, Fla., he smiled, exhaled audibly and said, "I'm sniffing the finish line." Gone, for the moment at least, was the melancholy slump of the shoulders and the guarded look in his eyes. Obama was leading in red states like Virginia and even threatening McCain in his home state of Arizona. The night before, some 35 million people had watched a powerful, if slick and gauzy, half-hour infomercial on Obama that aired in prime time on every network but ABC. The cost—$4 million—was a trifle for an organization that was outspending its opponent's campaign on TV by about three to one and had raised $150 million, a record amount for one month, in September. Axelrod had traded in his usual hiking boots for a pair of comfortable-looking slip-on loafers. He looked nearly presentable.

Speaking to a reporter a few days earlier, on Oct. 26, he had marveled at his opponents' missteps. He had been surprised by the choice of Palin. He called it an act of "message suicide," noting that the McCain campaign had spent the month of August trying to persuade voters to choose experience over celebrity, then "in one fell swoop they throw experience out the window, they hitch their wagon to this celebrity they're creating—and plainly [McCain] didn't put 'country first.'" Axelrod said he regretted "overreacting" to the "celebrity" ad in August, but when Palin gave McCain a brief surge in the polls in early September, he was happy that Obama had essentially ignored the advice of Democratic wise men, which he said was "You have to destroy her." His think-first instinct was standard Obama operating procedure. As he put it: "You can't judge the impact of the storm in the middle of the storm. You have to let the storm pass."

By this point, Axelrod's mind meld with Obama was so complete that the two men barely needed to speak. Eric

Holder recalled that from time to time during the deliberations over choosing a running mate, Obama would catch
Axelrod's eye, just for an instant, seeking some sign of ap-
probation or disapproval. Axelrod's phone would routinely
ring shortly before midnight, the hour when Obama liked to
do his deep thinking. (Axelrod would know it was Obama
calling by his ringtone: the tune to "Signed, Sealed, Delivered" by Stevie Wonder.)

It was hard to overstate Axelrod's feeling for the candidate.
When the political consultant had first met with Obama in
Chicago to discuss a potential presidential run in 2006,
Michelle had asked her husband what he could "uniquely"
contribute if he was elected. Obama answered that, right off
the bat, the day he was elected, "the world will look at us
differently—and I think a lot of young people across the
country will look at themselves differently."

To Axelrod, the romantic who read old Bobby Kennedy
speeches for fun, this was the sort of transformation that he
(along with a lot of '60s liberals) had spent his whole life
dreaming about. At the time of that meeting with the Obamas in 2006, Axelrod had been "so disgusted with the state
of politics, so disillusioned—we were about to elect a governor [Rod Blagojevich], he was an old client of mine and a
friend, but he was disappointing—I wanted to be involved in
something that reminded me of why I got into this work in
the first place," he recalled. On Sunday, Oct. 19, Axelrod had
been lying alone on his hotel bed watching *Meet the Press*
when Colin Powell movingly endorsed Obama. Axelrod had
thrust his fist in the air and became choked up.

Mark Salter, McCain's closest aide, had become increasingly isolated during the final weeks of the campaign. On the morning of the last debate, he had found the candidate stewing in his hotel room. McCain had become riled up after watching some conservative pundits on Fox urging him to lay into Obama that night. Campaign manager Rick Davis was also urging the candidate to take a more aggressive posture toward Obama on the Lewis comments. Davis argued that Obama had tried to bait Hillary Clinton, and she had called him out on it. Davis wanted McCain to do the same. Once again, Salter found himself as defender of the McCain brand, arguing that the candidate needed to stay dignified and not stoop to conquer. But McCain himself disagreed; he wanted to give Obama a chance to repudiate Lewis' comments. The discussion became heated. As he sometimes did when he was angry and frustrated, Salter stalked out of the room to have a cigarette.

The polls continued to look grim for McCain as the campaign entered the final weekend. He was trailing by an average of 8 points in 14 battleground states—falling further behind in nine and leading in none. On Halloween, a top McCain aide told a *Newsweek* reporter that McCain's odds of winning were roughly equal to "drawing to an inside royal flush." But McCain, who loved to joke "it's always darkest before it's completely black," seemed unflustered, even happy. His aides had seen this mood before. McCain did not mind being the underdog; he seemed to almost glory in battling for a lost cause. "The crazier things get, the calmer he becomes," said Matt McDonald, a senior adviser to McCain.

Salter was not surprised by McCain's attitude. Years before, McCain had told him how he idolized the character of Robert Jordan in Hemingway's *A Farewell to Arms*. Salter had written a chapter about Jordan in the book he coauthored with McCain, *Worth the Fighting For*. Salter (in McCain's voice, and clearly imagining McCain) described Jordan as "a man who would risk his life but never his honor." The title of the chapter was "Beautiful Fatalism," after a phrase Hemingway had used to describe warriors "who stayed loyal to a doomed cause." That pretty well described John McCain as he entered the last days of the long campaign.

On a bus trip through central Florida, McCain was tired but cheerful, exuberantly shaking hands with shoppers at an open-air market and humbly thanking a veteran of the Navy's submarine service. He made two brief, humorless statements to his former friends in the press. The crowds turned on the reporters, yelling, "When are you going to stop lying to America?" McCain-Palin supporters had embraced Joe the Plumber, and Palin, with her crowd sense, broadened the franchise to include Tito the Builder and Angela the Hairdresser (and Barack the Wealth Spreader). Irrepressible, Lindsey Graham had started calling his Senate pal "Joe the Biden," which McCain found inexplicably hilarious.

There wasn't much laughing on a bus ride through Pennsylvania. McCain sat alone in the back with his friend and aide Steve Duprey. "How are we doing in New Hampshire?" the candidate asked Duprey, who had been the New Hampshire

GOP chairman. McCain had a great fondness for the Granite State, where the independent-minded voters had given him overwhelming majorities in the Republican primaries in 2000 and 2008. Duprey hesitated, but looked McCain in the eye. "We're probably going to lose," he said. McCain looked genuinely shocked. "How did that happen?" the candidate asked, shaking his head. It wasn't just Obama, Duprey told him.

IN TRUTH, McCAIN'S "GROUND GAME," as the get-out-the-vote effort is sometimes called, was not strong. In many states, the McCain campaign was out-organized as well as outspent by Obama. Duprey believed that McCain's political director, Mike DuHaime, and the political operation did not understand New Hampshire. DuHaime, who had run the ill-fated Giuliani campaign, practiced off-the-shelf Republican red-meat politics. Duprey's own son had received a mailer highlighting McCain as pro-life. Duprey, like many New Hampshire Republicans, was pro-choice. Duprey told McCain, "I'm a supporter of Planned Parenthood. If they are mailing something like this to me, who else are they mistargeting?"

In a losing campaign, backbiting is inevitable. McCain knew this from his own experience. In 1996 he had played the role Lindsey Graham performed for him—he had ridden on the campaign plane as a friend/adviser to Bob Dole, the Kansas senator challenging President Bill Clinton. In the fall of '96, the Dole campaign had become a circular firing squad as the polls pointed to a Republican defeat. Indeed,

McCain himself had been one of those advisers occasionally second-guessing campaign strategy with reporters, even as he tried to counsel his buddy (and fellow wounded vet) Senator Dole. McCain did not want to read about his own campaign's infighting in the press. "Don't do that to me," he had told Salter and Schmidt, Davis and Charlie Black. And by and large they didn't. But especially as Schmidt brought in outsiders from the Bush-Cheney '04 campaign, the "unit cohesion," as McCain might put it, began to crumble.

On Sunday, Oct. 26, McCain's handlers had considered simply removing the Sunday Magazine from the candidate's copy of *The New York Times*, but McCain demanded the paper before anyone could remove the offending article. "The Making (and Remaking) of a Candidate," by Robert Draper, documented, in detail and with behind-the-curtain scenes, the many strategic lurches of McCain and his advisers. Before he was halfway through the 8,500-word article, McCain declared, quietly but firmly, "I'm very disappointed."

The discomfort among McCain's advisers was plain to see. Tensions had been building: in early October, as reporters trooped through the lobby of one hotel, they witnessed Salter and Nicolle Wallace arguing heatedly. Days later, Salter was unhappy with a statement by Wallace that seemed to defend the angry crowds stirred up by Governor Palin. Salter and Wallace clearly had a strained relationship. As reporters, who had been kept away from McCain, boarded the plane that day through the front door, they paraded past the candidate who was sitting on the couch that had been installed—but never used—for "Straight Talk" chats with the press. The candidate who had once traded japes with his press-corps pals did not even look up; he just looked glumly at the floor. He was flanked by Salter and Wallace, who stared grimly ahead.

Reporters noticed that Salter had been spending less and less time with his old pal Schmidt, and that Schmidt was more often seen in the company of Wallace. McCain's 24-year-old daughter Meghan was increasingly, and sometimes profanely, complaining that her father was being poorly served by his advisers. The atmosphere on the bus was becoming so poisonous that one midlevel staffer e-mailed another to say, "Kill me." And yet, as the odds grew longer and Election Day grew closer, Salter took his cue from McCain, or perhaps from their shared mythic doppelgänger, Robert Jordan. Salter stopped brooding and began joking around, as if he were mocking the fates. To the theme tune from *Rocky*, the music used to introduce McCain as the fighting underdog at rallies, Salter entertained staffers with a shadowboxing match with Schmidt. The latter became a little overenthusiastic, however, and clipped Salter's aviator glasses, slightly cutting and bruising Salter's eye socket. When reporters asked what had happened, Salter pointed to the small wound and joked, "Vicious staff infighting."

The sharpest jabs were aimed at Palin. An anonymous McCain staffer described her to Politico as "wacko" and a "diva." When Politico reported on Oct. 21 that Palin had spent $150,000 for clothes for herself and her family, the governor had been all wounded innocence. At a campaign stop in Tampa, she said, "These clothes—they're not my property, just like the lighting and the staging and everything else that the RNC purchased. I am not taking them with me. I am back to wearing clothes from my favorite consignment shop in Anchorage, Alaska." Publicly, McCain aides backed up Palin, saying that a third of the clothes had been returned immediately, before they were worn in public, and that the rest would be donated to charity. Privately, however, McCain's top advisers fumed at what they regarded as Palin's outrageous profligacy. One senior aide said that Nicolle Wallace had told Palin to buy three suits for the convention and hire a stylist, but thereafter Palin had "gone rogue," as the media buzz put it. She began buying for herself and her family—clothes and accessories from top stores like Saks Fifth Avenue and Neiman Marcus. A week after she announced that she was going back to her consignment shop she was still having tailored clothes delivered. According to two knowledgeable sources, a vast majority of the clothes were bought by a wealthy donor, who was shocked when he got the bill. Palin also used low-level staffers to buy some of the clothes on their credit cards; the McCain campaign found out when the aides sought reimbursement. One aide estimated that she spent "tens of thousands" more than the reported $150,000, and that $20,000 to $40,000 went to buy clothes for her husband. Some articles of clothing have apparently been lost. An angry aide characterized the shopping spree as "Wasilla Hillbillies looting Neiman Marcus from coast to coast" and said the truth will eventually come out when the Republican Party audits its books. A Palin aide said: "Governor Palin was not directing staffers to put anything on their personal credit cards, and anything that staffers put on their credit cards has been reimbursed, like an expense. Nasty and false accusations following a defeat say more about the person who made them than they do about Governor Palin." The aide added, "It's incredibly egregious that you even consider running this."

On the last full day of campaigning, Monday, Nov. 3, Obama walked out onstage and surveyed the crowd for a few extra seconds before giving his stump speech. The crowd was in a festive mood. A middle-aged woman with a silk scarf salsa-danced with a beaming Latino man, holding both hands above his head and flashing the victory sign as he spun and gyrated to the song "Ain't No Stopping Us Now." Reporters, who rarely budged from the laptops in the press room to hear Obama deliver his well-worn speech, streamed toward the stage to get a better view of the candidate. They seemed to sense that the long campaign was finally over, that this was their last chance to see the political phenomenon, who rarely came back to talk to the press. "I have just one word for you, Florida," Obama declared to the crowd. "Tomorrow." He drew on the oratory of the civil-rights movement, intoning, "We have a righteous wind at our backs."

That morning, Obama talked by phone to Michelle in Chicago and learned that his grandmother, Madelyn Dunham, had died. He had broken off the campaign the week before to fly to her bedside in Honolulu, and he was glad to have had the chance to say goodbye to the woman he called "Toot" (after Tutu, the Hawaiian word for grandmother). Late in the afternoon, standing before 25,000 people in Charlotte, N.C., he mentioned his grandmother's passing. "She has gone home," he said. His voice grew hoarse, and he called his grandmother a "silent hero," one of many silent heroes who toil in obscurity to create better lives for their families. Unlike presidents Reagan, Clinton and both Bushes—who all readily choked up or shed tears—Obama rarely showed any emotion. But now he reached into a pocket, pulled out a handkerchief and dabbed his face, wet with tears.

On election morning, Obama voted at home in Chicago and flew to Indiana. He made a surprise stop at a union hall serving as an Election Day canvassing center and phone bank. "Hey, guys!" he said brightly as he entered the room. The candidate began taking the phone from the hands of phone-bank callers and catching several voters on the other end of the line by surprise. Then it was off to the gym for his ritual basketball game.

At Obama headquarters at 233 North Michigan Avenue, there was the usual profusion of pizza boxes and harried-looking staffers. But the finance bullpen was empty. The mighty Obama money machine was finally silent; its staff had been sent to the states to work the polls. In the boiler room on the 19th floor (bare concrete floors and swatches of industrial carpet duct-taped to the floor over bundles of wires and cables snaking underneath some 20 tables), special desks had been set up for every battleground state—ready to respond to a low turnout or unleash a flood of robo-calls. But at 3 P.M. on Election Day, with polls open across the country, a spot check revealed no burgeoning crises, no surprises, only minor problems swiftly dealt with. If anything, the staff, primed for trouble on every front, was pleasantly surprised to find little of it. The "boiler room" seemed like a misnomer. The bloodless, businesslike atmosphere had the feel of a corporate office on a slow Tuesday, not a political war room on decision day.

At the very end, the Reverend Wright did make an appearance. An independent expenditure group called the National Republican Trust PAC ran an ad on *Saturday Night Live*'s prime-time election special. The ad attacking Obama's former pastor was slick, with much better production values than the crude Reverend Wright videos running on the Internet. But it was too little, too late. When a *Newsweek* reporter e-mailed a top Obama adviser for reaction, a reply came back reading simply: ZZZZZ.

MCCAIN INSISTED ON A FINAL town hall in New Hampshire. His aides wanted a brief rally near the airport in Manchester (New Hampshire has only four electoral votes, and the campaign wanted to move on to bigger states), but McCain insisted on the long bus ride to Peterborough, a rustic town like the many where McCain had—twice, in 1999 and 2007—created political momentum from nothing. On the ride, he joked with New Hampshire friends and Joe Lieberman about the fun times in New Hampshire—dragging voters to town halls when he stood at zero in the polls. New Hampshire adviser Mike Dennehy later said that McCain's town-hall event in Peterborough was his "best event in New Hampshire, probably ever." Afterward, when McCain boarded the plane, he turned to Dennehy and said, "How many are we down by?" Dennehy looked at him for a second. "Let's not talk about that tonight," Dennehy said.

On the last flight home to Arizona, McCain came back to say goodbye to the reporters he had long since virtually stopped speaking to, still stunned by what he viewed as personal betrayal by friends in the press corps. "Feelin' good, feelin' confident about the way things have turned out," the candidate said, delivering the necessary white lie. "We've spent a lot of time together. . . . We've had a great time. I wish all of you every success and look forward to being with you in the future." Behind him, Cindy McCain did not disguise her feelings. She teared up and looked drained. So did McCain's traveling buddies Lieberman and Lindsey Graham.

Steve Schmidt spoke briefly with the reporters. "Are you happy with the campaign?" he was asked. He answered: "I think we did our absolute best in really difficult circumstances. . . . It is highly doubtful that anyone will have to run in a worse political climate than the one John McCain had to run in this year." Another reporter asked if he was happy with "the pick of Palin." He ducked the question. Schmidt was trying, not very hard, to hide his true feelings. He had been compelled to personally take over Palin's debate prep when she seemed unwilling to engage in the drudge work of learning the issues. McCain's advisers had been frustrated when Palin refused to talk to donors because she found it corrupting, and they were furious when they heard rumors that Todd Palin was calling around to Alaska bigwigs telling them to hold their powder until 2012. The day of the third debate, Palin refused to go onstage with New Hampshire GOP Sen. John Sununu and Jeb Bradley, a former New Hampshire congressman running for a House seat, because their views on abortion didn't fully align and because Bradley had earlier opposed drilling in Alaska. (He changed his position during the race). The McCain campaign ordered her onstage at the next campaign stop, but she refused to acknowledge the two Republican candidates standing behind her. McCain himself rarely spoke to Palin (perhaps once a week when they were not traveling together, estimated one adviser). Aides kept him in the dark about Palin's spending on clothes because they were sure he'd be offended. In his concession speech, McCain praised Palin, but the body language between them onstage was not particularly friendly. (Palin had asked to speak; Schmidt vetoed the request.)

McCain's speech, written by Salter, could not have been more gracious to Obama. It evoked McCain's life of service with humility and reminded voters what McCain's campaign might have been. He said he had no regrets. "Today," he said, "I was a candidate for the highest office in the country I love so much. And tonight, I remain her servant. That is blessing enough for anyone . . . "

On election night, Obama ate a steak dinner with his family at their home in Chicago's Hyde Park. Repairing to a hotel suite, he closeted himself with the core group that had been with him from the beginning—Axelrod, Plouffe, communications director Robert Gibbs and Valerie Jarrett, his family friend and mentor. Various children—Obama's two girls, the children of Michelle's brother Craig, Gibbs's son, Joe Biden's grandchildren—happily wandered in and out. For most of the fall, the campaign had worried about Ohio as the most important battleground state. When the news came through that Obama had won Ohio, Obama said to Axelrod, "So it looks like we're going to win this thing, huh?" Axelrod replied, "It looks like it, yeah." He deadpanned, "I don't want to congratulate you until I can congratulate you." According to Jarrett, Obama was "as even-tempered as ever."

In a sea of Americans in Grant Park in Chicago at midnight, Obama said, "It has been a long time coming, but tonight, because of what we did on this day, in this election, at this defining moment, change has come to America." Yes, it has.

Obama's victory caused elation across America and around the world. (Photo by Chip Somodevilla / Getty Images)

Epilogue

In the days after the election, if became fashionable to compare Barack Obama to Abraham Lincoln. *The New Yorker* magazine showed a rising moon (the "o" in *New Yorker*) shining on the Lincoln Memorial, and *Newsweek* linked the names of Lincoln and Obama on its cover. Two thin men from rude beginnings, relatively new to Washington but wise to the world, bring the nation together to face a crisis. Both men superb rhetoricians, both geniuses at stagecraft and timing. Obama, like Lincoln and unlike most modern politicians, even wrote his own speeches, or at least drafted the really important ones—by hand, on yellow legal paper—such as his remarkably honest speech on race during the Reverend Wright imbroglio in the spring of 2008.

Obama did have a talented young speechwriter named Jon Favreau, and on the day before the election, Favreau worked up a draft of a victory speech and sent it to Obama. The word came back from Obama's chief strategist, David Axelrod, who was sitting with Obama in Charlotte, N.C.: "Barack wants to lean into bipartisanship a little more. Even though the Democrats have won a great victory, we should reach out and be humbled by it. Figure out a good Lincoln quote to bring it all together," advised Axelrod, who suggested looking at the end of Lincoln's first Inaugural Address.

More than familiar with Lincoln's rhetoric, Favreau decided to pass on the most overquoted passage of all, invoking "the better angels of our nature," and to quote the words that came before: "We are not enemies, but friends. . . . Though passion may have strained, it must not break our bonds of affection."

To a public thoroughly sick of partisan bickering, these words rang with hope as Obama spoke them on election night. If there was any one message that defined the Obama campaign from the beginning, it was his promise to rise above the petty politics of division and unite the country. But as Obama met with possible cabinet secretaries at his home in Chicago, he had to contemplate political reality. The newly elected Congress would be left of center, particularly the old liberal bulls that chair committees and form much of the leadership of the House and Senate. The country, on the other hand, remained right of center (exit polls on Election Day showed that 22 percent of voters identify themselves as liberal, 33 percent as conservative and 46 percent as moderate) or at least more moderate than left. Especially in the Senate, where the Democrats stood to be perhaps one vote shy of the 60 needed to break a filibuster and pass a bill, compromise and coalition-building would be the order of the day. If Obama was to accomplish much of anything, he would need all the leadership skills of a Lincoln.

The theme of Obama's Inauguration would be taken from a line in Lincoln's Gettysburg Address: "A New Birth of Freedom." Asked in January of 2008 by CBS anchor Katie Couric which book, aside from the Bible, he would find essential in the Oval Office, Obama had answered, *Team of Rivals*. Doris Kearns Goodwin's 2005 bestseller recounts how Lincoln surrounded himself with advisers who were better educated and more experienced and who made no secret of coveting Lincoln's job. As Obama mulled his cabinet picks, he was looking at some strong personalities, such as Larry Summers as an economic advisor, and he was strongly considering keeping on Bush's secretary of defense, Robert Gates, which he decided to do in December. Bursting with ego, Rahm Emanuel, Obama's pick as White House chief of staff, did not at all fit the "No Drama" Obama mode of the campaign. Emanuel once sent a foe a dead fish wrapped in newspaper.

The most intriguing development to emerge in the two weeks after election day was the strong possibility that Hillary Clinton would become secretary of state. She flew to Chicago to meet with Obama, and word quickly leaked out that she was Obama's first choice. The sticking point appeared to be Hillary's husband, the former president, who had to agree to sharply limit his overseas travel and fund raising. Bill Clinton said he was willing to do whatever was necessary, but there were more than a few Washington observers who wondered whether he could take a non-disruptive role in the new regime. The rumors proved true, and Hillary accepted Obama's nomination in early December.

During the Civil War, Lincoln was able to brilliantly manage his team of rivals. His secretary of state, William Seward, came into office thinking "he would actually be controlling Lincoln," noted Goodwin, but Lincoln was able to sit Seward down, remind him who was president—and ultimately make him his close friend. Lincoln, in some ways, had it easier than Obama. Cabinet secretaries in the 1860s could not step out on the White House lawn and hold press conferences with cable-TV networks. But Goodwin, who had spoken with Obama about her book, believed that he had absorbed the deeper meaning of Lincoln's leadership style. "I think he's got a temperamental set of qualities that have some resemblance to Lincoln's emotional intelligence," Goodwin told *Newsweek*.

THE MOST IMPORTANT QUALITY may be humility, which both Obama and Lincoln often counted as an essential virtue. Humility in this case is not to be confused with meekness or passivity. Rather, it comes from confidence. A Lincolnesque leader is confident enough to be humble—to not feel the need to bluster or dominate, but to be sufficiently sure of one's own judgment and self-worth to really listen and not be threatened by contrary advice. Lincoln showed this rare quality before he was sworn into office in March 1861. "Lincoln wrote a really bellicose Inaugural [Address] at home," says Harold Holzer, author of *Lincoln President-Elect*. "It ended with looking at the South and saying, 'Shall it be peace or sword?' He showed the draft to people, and they all urged him to tone it down and make it more conciliatory." And so he did. It turns out that the sentiment quoted by Obama in Grant Park ("We are not enemies, but friends . . .") was suggested, in words close to those used by Lincoln, by his rival Seward.

Obama, as ever, could be cocky. During the campaign, he liked to appear onstage alone—"the One," as Oprah Winfrey blessed him—without the usual scenes of families and party pooh-bahs and hangers-on. But Obama was self-aware. In his book, *The Audacity of Hope*, he describes how he rather grandly wrote in the pages of *Time* magazine, "In Lincoln's rise from poverty, his ultimate mastery of language and law, his capacity to overcome personal loss and remain determined in the face of repeated defeat—in all this, he reminded me not just of my own struggles." Recalling the episode, Obama goes on to ruefully note that he was zinged by columnist Peggy Noonan in *The Wall Street Journal*: "This week comes the previously careful Sen. Barack Obama, flapping his wings in *Time* magazine and explaining that he's a lot like Abraham Lincoln, only sort of better." Writes Obama: "Ouch!"

Obama has unusual detachment for a politician. He observes himself as a kind of figure out of literature. Walking the streets of Springfield, the Illinois state capital, on the day he was speaking at the dedication of the Lincoln library, he "started wondering," as he put it, whether "the poor boy born in the backwoods of Kentucky ever dreamed" that a presidential library would be dedicated in his name—or that it was possible "for a black man [Obama] to speak at that dedication as a United States Senator." As a senator, Obama writes in *Audacity*, he liked to jog on warm evenings down the Mall to the Lincoln Memorial, where he stood and silently mouthed the words carved in marble.

He writes of going to the White House, of visiting the Lincoln Bedroom: "A modest space with antique furniture, a four-poster bed, an original copy of the Gettysburg Address discreetly displayed under glass—and a big, flat-screen TV set atop one of the desks. Who, I wondered, flipped on *SportsCenter* while spending the night in the Lincoln Bedroom?" At a White House breakfast meeting with some other senators, he describes President Bush as a kind of anti-Lincoln. Dealing with the question of judicial appointments, writes Obama, "the President's eyes became fixed; his voice took on the agitated, rapid tone of someone neither accustomed to nor welcoming interruption; his easy affability was replaced by an almost messianic certainty."

By contrast, Obama praises Lincoln's "practicality," "that self-awareness, that humility." And yet, apparently without sensing any irony, on the very next page of his book, Obama records how he "declined to be a part of what would be called the Gang of Fourteen." The Gang of 14 was a bipartisan group of senators that tried to break through partisan deadlock over judicial appointments. As a senator, Obama showed a notable unwillingness to take political risks by reaching across the aisle on controversial matters (in contrast to his presidential opponent, John McCain, who routinely sought bipartisan coalitions and was one of the Gang of 14).

Former House speaker Newt Gingrich was a self-described "student of Lincoln" and author of two books on the Civil War. In an interview with *Newsweek*, Gingrich said he was impressed by Obama's use of Lincoln as a prop. But he was waiting to see if Obama would be sincere in his emulation.

"Obama's got a liberal voting record, and I don't know of any substantive issue where he's ever broken with his leadership," said Gingrich. Obama had friends across the aisle—including Sen. Dick Lugar of Indiana and Sen. Tom Coburn of Oklahoma. Mentioned as a possible secretary of state, Lugar hinted that he was not interested (he spoke with Obama shortly after the election; the conversation was kept private). Two weeks after the election, Coburn's staff told *Newsweek* that he had yet to hear from Obama or anyone on his staff.

GINGRICH SAID AN EARLY TEST of whether Obama was a centrist or beholden to liberal interest groups would come on the "card-check bill." Labor unions have long wanted a law that would do away with secret balloting and allow labor organizers to lean on workers to sign a statement demanding a union (the card check). Obama had said he would support such a provision, which would infuriate big business and free marketers. (One prominent Democrat, asking for anonymity to not antagonize organized labor, said that Obama should let the unions have their way on the card-check bill—but only to temporize, to keep the unions from demanding protectionist legislation that would be even more harmful to the economy.)

Obama was sure to come under pressure from progressives to push the big-ticket items in the Democratic platform, like universal health care. The new president faced a basic choice, said William Galston, former policy adviser in the Clinton administration: "Do you put the pedal to the metal or do you say, 'We've had a big victory, sure we could push anything through, but we're not going to do that for the sake of unity'?" He cautioned against option A. "If you go for broke, you may go broke," he said. A shrewder course would be to win some easy victories early on and build momentum for the hard choices later. Obama would certainly have to back a big stimulus package to counter the deepening recession. Since lawmakers like to spend money, and even conservatives saw a need to boost the economy, a massive spending bill did not appear difficult to get through Congress (harder would be to make it smart spending—getting the money to people who can spend it quickly—rather than pet pork-barrel projects that take too much time or spending programs that can't be turned off when the recession ends).

Obama took a few early steps to show that he was above partisanship and score-settling. In the Senate, the Democratic leadership threatened to boot Sen. Joe Lieberman, McCain's travelling buddy, out of his chairmanship of the homeland-security committee. Obama communicated to Senate Majority Leader Harry Reid that he wanted to let bygones be bygones and allow Lieberman to keep his chairmanship. Reid backed down.

Two weeks after Election Day, McCain met with Obama in Washington. The talk was scheduled for 90 minutes but lasted only 40. The two men did not exactly bond, but it seemed more likely that McCain would be a friend than an enemy in the months ahead. A top adviser to McCain told *Newsweek* that McCain "showed no bitterness whatsoever" over the election results, and that he would likely play the role of deal-maker and conciliator in the Senate. "There will come a time when Obama is tested by international crisis and the Russians or someone will jump in the gap to criticize him, and John McCain will emerge to tell the country that the president is doing the right thing," predicted the adviser.

Obama made clear that he wanted a bipartisan look and cast to his administration. The transition team was told to hire Republicans at all levels of government, not just as token cabinet appointments. "'Team of Rivals' has become a term of art here," said a senior Obama staffer. "It's less about Lincoln than a reinforcement of his theme that we need to move forward and get beyond the old partisan politics." This staffer said that Obama and his top aides were wary of over-hyping the Lincoln comparison. He also said that Obama believed he could—by force of character—bring Republicans into the fold without sacrificing Democratic principles. "I don't think he looks at this and says, 'Because I appoint Republicans, I have to compromise my positions,'" said the aide.

Perhaps, but it was obvious that Obama would have to broker compromises to take on really tough challenges, like dependence on foreign oil. For instance, he may have to go along with drilling for oil off America's shores as part of a deal to limit consumption of carbon fuels. One of these days, a president will have to tackle the cost of entitlement programs like Medicare and Social Security. Obama might be the one—if he is to keep the federal deficit from spiraling so far out of control that debt payments jerk up interest rates.

If Obama was to establish some momentum—if he was to restore public trust in government, a very tall order—he'd have more luck asking for sacrifice later on. Of course, any strategy or timetable is likely to run up against unexpected events. A foreign crisis or a terrorist attack would absorb Obama's energies and perhaps even change his basic course (think of President Bush's transformation after 9/11).

When history is written, advisers like to play up their roles. But in truth, the American presidency is a lonely job; the really big decisions must be made by the president alone. Though Obama preferred to model himself on Lincoln, or perhaps FDR, another close comparison could be made to Lyndon Johnson. Like Obama, LBJ closely questioned his aides and wanted to hear the truth. "He would cross-examine you," recalls Francis Bator, LBJ's deputy national-security adviser. But then it was very hard to tell what LBJ was really thinking or what he'd ultimately do. Some Obama advisers noticed the same trait in the president-elect. He could be hard to read; he was, in the end, a very self-contained and rather solitary figure. With luck, he would not be confronted with lose-lose decisions like LBJ, who had to choose between the Great Society and the war in Vietnam and ultimately lost both. Obama will surely face some hard choices, and possibly all at once. He may not wind up as a tragic figure like LBJ, but he may also disappoint the expectations of his vast legions of believers. He will not be "the One"; he will be human like the rest of us.

Still, when the forty-fourth president is inaugurated on Jan. 20, and he mounts a platform that looks west, down the Mall and toward the Lincoln Memorial honoring the sixteenth president, he could do worse than ask himself: what would Lincoln do?

*Obama and his expanded Democratic majority in Congress now face
the challenge of guiding the country through a tumultuous period.*

An Interview with Barack Obama

I**N MAY OF 2008**, I interviewed Democratic presidential candidate Barack Obama during a campaign flight from Oregon to Chicago. It had taken months to secure the interview—months during which Obama and his team had put off my requests to interview him for this book. I wanted to step back from the daily churn of the campaign and talk big-picture stuff: how Obama had decided to run, what had made him think, at the outset, that he could best Hillary Clinton, how he and the campaign had weathered some rough going in the early months of the campaign. To this point, my requests had fallen on unsympathetic ears. "We're trying to win a nomination," I'd been told repeatedly, and it was hard to argue with that—I'd seen firsthand what a grueling campaign schedule Obama had and how completely full his days were, from before dawn to well after midnight most days. Finally, though, the campaign relented, and I thought I knew why. Just a few days before, with the number of primary contests dwindling, and Hillary needing a game-changing turn of fortune, Obama had carried the North Carolina primary by nearly 15 percentage points, and had fought Clinton to a near-draw in Indiana, where she won by a single point. "We now know who the Democratic nominee is going to be, and no one is going to dispute it," Tim Russert said that night.

"Come on up," said Robert Gibbs, Obama's spokesman, waving me to the front section of Obama's campaign plane. The invitation was as much an indication as I'd get that the campaign was feeling optimistic. Although Obama had already started talking about the general election and recalibrating his stump speech to focus less on Clinton, more on McCain, there were no outward signs of celebration—it was business as usual within a very businesslike campaign. Gibbs escorted me to Obama's first-class row, where the senator sat at the window, reading a copy of *The New Yorker*. Obama looked up, said hello, and asked me to sit. On the advice of one of Obama's best friends, who thought that Obama would respond well to my somewhat unconventional path into journalism, I started to tell him a bit about my background, but I had stumbled over only a couple of awkward sentences when Obama broke in and said, "I have a suggestion. Why don't you just ask me some questions? I want to make sure you maximize your time. You don't need to make me feel comfortable with you; if I didn't trust you, you wouldn't be here." I was immediately struck by Obama's focus, so intense that it almost felt like a physical force.

By this point in the campaign, I'd seen Obama interviewed dozens of times, and heard him answer hundreds, if not thousands of questions. After some early struggles, he'd almost mastered campaign-speak, the dull art of condensing any answer to any question into a talking point. But as we began to talk, it quickly became apparent that he wasn't in campaign mode. Away from the unblinking eyes of the TV cameras that tracked him at every debate, and from the brace of microphones at every campaign stop that recorded his every utterance, later to be pored over for any gaffe or possible gaffe, Obama seemed more at ease. His speech fell into the natural pattern that his advisers had tried to drum out of him, full of pensive pauses and compound sentences. At one point, when I asked Obama what more he'd asked of himself, during a difficult stretch in the campaign where he'd asked his team to redouble their efforts, he paused for a full seventeen seconds before answering. Obama is fiercely intelligent and characteristically confident, but what I remember most was how self-aware he seemed, with a grasp of his own strengths as well as weaknesses and a keen sense of other people's reactions to him. I found the interview fascinating—a revealing glimpse into a man who I suspect even then had a quiet confidence that he would be the nation's next president.

—DAREN BRISCOE

[Some of the questions have been edited for conciseness and clarity, and extraneous material omitted.]

Q: Going back to the period where you were deciding whether to run or not, I'm very curious about what you wanted to hear when you sat around with your friends and advisers. What were you looking for in terms of what you hoped to hear from them?

Obama: Well, the first question was, could I win? And I think that's something that I needed to get some very objective assessments of, because one of the things that I've always been suspicious of is the hype that surrounded my entry into the U.S. Senate. I wanted to make sure that we hadn't fallen prey to hype and believing our own press, so I wanted to test in very concrete terms and push very hard on the question of whether we could win. Since we assumed that we had a strong field, including Sen. Clinton and John Edwards.

The second question, which had more to do with conversations between Michelle and myself on which we needed some feedback from the staff who had been through a presidential election, was how it would have an impact on our family. And that actually was the most important question, but unless we crossed the threshold where we could win, the second one became moot, because I had no interest in running if I didn't think we could win. I wasn't interested in setting myself up for four years from now because to some degree I was very fortunate; I already had a very high profile. I stood to lose more than gain in a presidential race if I wasn't successful. So the second question was: how it would affect our family? And then thinking about schedules and workloads and the rhythm of a campaign, the nature of the scrutiny involved, how it would alter our daily round, and how would we, how effectively could we shield our families, our girls?

And then the third question, which was the most profound question, and one where probably . . . in the end I had to answer all by myself was: should I win? Just because you can win doesn't mean you're the person who's best for the country at this moment in time, and I, I, I actually believe my own rhetoric when I say I think we're in a defining moment. It's very difficult to think back to a time where we had a bigger series of choices, and obviously WWII maybe, and then the immediate aftermath of WWII, the Great Depression, and before that, the Civil War . . . but the country has a lot of issues that it's got to deal with. And so I don't, I didn't think it was sufficient for me to run just because of my own ambition or because I thought this was my time. I felt as if there had to be at least the possibility that I could do something that no other candidate in the race could do, whether it was bringing the country together more effectively, [or] building a consensus, [or] reinvigorating the American people's interest in government. So that was a series of questions that had to be raised, and those questions were probably the ones that were least amenable to quantification. I mean, we can do some polling and sort of figure out, "Alright, can we win this thing or not?" It's a lot harder to gauge whether you are what the country needs at this point in time.

Q: Were there any points, either in the conversations with your friends, or in the conversations with Michelle, or in the conversations with yourself, anything now that stands out in your mind as crossing the threshold, where you went from "Well, maybe not" to "Maybe so"?

Obama: Well, one critical moment was where Michelle said that she would be willing to do it.

Q: And her biggest hesitation was concern about the impact on your family, or concern for your safety?

Obama: Mostly the impact on the family—the impact on her, the impact on the girls, my absence, our loss of privacy. Michelle is not somebody who defines herself by my political success or defines our family by my political success. She's much more interested in me being a good father, and her having support, our kids doing well, and so her belief that this was worth it and that our family could manage the stresses and strains was probably the most important piece to the puzzle. I think a second part, the second piece to the puzzle, was her conclusion that I could win, that I wasn't the odds on favorite, but that it was possible for me to pull this off. And I think the final piece was the sense that there were no guarantees, but I might just be able to break through the partisanship, the gridlock that had existed for the last 20 years, and offer a fresh perspective in our politics at a time when our country needed a clean break from the past.

Q: When Michelle was processing this and grappling with this question herself, what role did you take? Did you give her space? Did she have questions for you?

Obama: She had questions, but her initial instinct was to say no. Her initial instinct was that we had just gotten off of the U.S. Senate campaign, we had finally stabilized a little bit, the girls were getting older, she knew how difficult it was for me to be away from the girls, she feels lonely when I'm not around, so her initial instinct was not to do it. And I think she also felt that the Clintons were tough and that I would be subject to a lot of attacks. She felt that eight years later I would be in a stronger position and less vulnerable to attack. She doesn't like to see her husband attacked.

Q: Now you're a pretty persuasive guy. Did you do much in the way of trying to persuade her, or did you just leave it with her and let her find her way?

Obama: We just talked it through. It wasn't as if it was a slam-dunk for me. I think part of the reason she agreed to do it was because she knew that she had veto power, that she and the girls ultimately mattered more than my own ambitions in this process, and that if she said no, we would be ok.

Q: The point at which she said ok, do you remember that well?

Obama: No. I'm sure, by the way, that she was influenced by other people, who might have been stronger advocates for the notion that now is the time, than even I was.

Q: There had to have been some range of opinion amongst the people close to you about whether it was a good idea. Can you give me any sense of who was where? Do you have an institutional skeptic among your friends?

Obama: I think everybody just tried to be as objective as possible. I think we all were of the same mindset, which was, this will be a daunting and difficult task, and there is a high price to it, but it may be worth it, and so I think it was a very systematic deliberation, it wasn't as if there were two people who were saying yes, and two people who were saying no, and I was weighing it back and forth. I think everybody was a mix of yes and no. Everybody was excited about the prospect of mounting a campaign. I think everybody had an instinct that the country might be looking for something new, but everybody I think was also mindful that the odds weren't in our favor and that it would exact a significant personal toll.

Q: Give me your own sense of the Clintons and how they factored into your own decision. You said that Michelle was worried about them and knew they were tough, and I'm sure you thought they were tough too, but in deciding that you were going to run, clearly you must have decided that you could take them.

Obama: Well . . . my view of the Clintons has always been generally favorable. As I've written in my book, I think that Bill Clinton was a very important figure in helping to steer the Democratic party out of the wilderness. I think he's as smart and effective a politician as we've seen. You know, he and I sort of have roughly similar perspectives on where . . . let me put it this way, I think he is instinctively a pragmatist and not an ideologue, and so I think we share some sympathies there. And with respect to Hillary, I've always viewed her as extraordinarily smart, as disciplined a person as I've ever seen . . . a more effective communicator than she is given credit for. My instinct was, though, that given all of their history, they could not reset the country, they could not move us past some of the old arguments. And so . . . it wasn't so much that I didn't think Senator Clinton could win, which some people have voiced. It was more of an assessment of whether she would be able to govern and move the big issues forward. My assessment was that they were going to be very tough because they had a 20-year head start in building a political operation that was as good as anything out there.

Q: Yet, even taking that into consideration, you still gave yourself a shot.

Obama: You know, this isn't all science. Some of it is just feeling. And there was a feeling that the country was searching for something. And we could see it. I had done my book signing in October, and there was just this remarkable, visceral response, not all of it justified by me, it was more . . . that I had become a symbol for the next thing. So some of it was undeserved, but what it told me was that people really were looking for something different. I joked with my team—and it wasn't entirely a joke, it's something I still think about—that the country was looking for a Barack Obama. Now, I'm not sure that I *am* Barack Obama, right? But they were looking for an idea like that. It was an idea that we're moving into a different phase of politics, and we're moving past the old racial divisions, and we're moving past some of the sharply ideological arguments, and we're trying to, in a very practical, concrete, common sense way, solve some problems that we can't put off any longer, and that we've got to try to be real honest with the American people about this and treat them like adults. I always felt as if I were an imperfect vessel for that idea, but I have a pretty strong instinct that that particular message might resonate with the American people right now.

Q: And you had that instinct before you went on the book signing tour . . .

Obama: Yes.

Q: . . . and the tour sort of validated that?

Obama: I mean, it was an instinct I had when I ran for the United States Senate.

Q: Let's talk about the summer after you guys got in the race, about that period where the feeling was that you guys were kind of in the doldrums . . .

Obama: Let's back up. . . . Before we get there, a couple of things happened. Number one, we were stunned with our fundraising success. Keep in mind that we basically outraised [Hillary Clinton] in that first quarter, something that nobody expected, least of all, me. And so, in some ways, that created a set of outsized expectations. I think everybody was shocked, and having set the bar real high, suddenly we were no longer the underdogs we expected to be. The sense was that somehow we were this phenomenon, and the hype built around that in what I think was an unhealthy way, because I was still learning my way. The same thing happened, by the way, in our rallies. . . . Just in those first couple of months after the announcement, none of us thought we'd have 17,000 people at the announcement, in seven degree weather. In that first couple of months, it was like we defied gravity. We got 23,000 people in Austin, Texas, the month after I had announced.

And that did a couple of things. It confirmed my instinct that the country really was hungry for something fresh and new. On the other hand, it put us immediately in the spotlight at a time when we were still trying to work out the kinks of our organization, and I was certainly trying to work out the kinks of my own presentation. My stump speech back then . . . people would see these huge crowds and all the reporters were writing, "Oh his stump is kind of uninspired." Well, what I had done in my U.S. Senate race was develop my stump organically. I wouldn't necessarily write it all down. I'd try different things and refine them until it really worked. The difference in the Senate race was, I had six months where I was just talking to crowds of 50 people and 100 people, or I was in somebody's living room, without a camera. Suddenly, day one [of the campaign], people are thinking, "Every time he comes out we want him to be as good as he was at the convention speech." And that was a speech I had taken three weeks or four weeks to write and had memorized. So I think that caught us off guard.

I remember that there was an SEIU health care forum, and it was before the first debate. And all the candidates were just supposed to be presenting our views on health care. And because our policy team wasn't all that well worked out, I had a pretty good sense of where I wanted to go on health care, but we hadn't unveiled our health care plan . . . we went in there a little casual. I sat down and had kind of a general conversation about health care the way I would if I were on Charlie Rose or something, and you know, Hillary was standing up, and she gave a full-blown presentation. And Edwards had already come out with his plan and was very specific about what he wanted to do. We just got ripped in the press, "Oh look, Obama; he's unprepared; he's amateurish."

So what happened was, we were very successful in fundraising, very successful in building big crowds, had a terrific rollout, but suddenly expectations were up to here [raising his left hand head-high] and we were still, we still had an off-Broadway mentality except we were on the Great White Way. So we had a lot of catching up to do. And that, that tendency to set expectations very high for us, very early on, would continue all the way into the summer, and into the debates. . . . If you've never been involved in a presidential debate before, I don't care who you are, you're going to be a little guarded, a little awkward, and a little uncertain. . . . When I was asked about terrorism, and I didn't immediately say I'd bomb the heck out of somebody, that was sort of jumped upon by the pundits [who said]: "Look, this is an example [of his awkwardness]." . . . It wasn't even that my answer was wrong; it was that it showed that I hadn't been in the national spotlight long enough to know that you've got to signify your toughness by blowing somebody up first before you start taking care of the wounded in the event of a terrorist attack. And so it was that we got some very rapid lessons in presidential politics, very quickly.

Q: I'm reminded of reading about you when you went to go play [basketball] with these guys at the University of North

Carolina. You got out there for a while and you said, "These guys are big, and they're fast," and it took you a little while to get up to game speed. Was there some of that?

Obama: No, it was a little bit different from that, because there was no phase in the campaign where I watched the other candidates and said to myself, "Wow, look at what they're doing." . . . We were still in training camp, but in terms of the press' perspective, the game had already begun. And you know, John Edwards had been campaigning for two years at that point. Hillary had essentially been planning for her campaign for a very long time. And those were the two I was being compared to because of our hype and because of the money being raised. And so for me it was more just watching and saying, "All right, the game has started. They've got a head start; we've got to catch up."

Q: And was this the point at which it was said—I'm not sure whether you said it first or someone else said it—but where you made the point, "Hey, we've got to step our game up"?

Obama: Well . . . I don't remember exactly the timetable. . . . The one thing I did understand—and this was from my Senate race, where we were in third place for the entire contest until the last month—what I did understand was that in politics, six months, nine months is an eternity, and so I wasn't nervous about all this. My attitude was let's just keep on building and learning and improving, and everybody stay steady. There wasn't a lot of shouting or hollering, it was just, "Let's each day get a little bit better and make steady progress."

Q: But it appears as though there was a recalibration at some point, maybe an adjustment in your own organization's assessment of what it was going to take . . .

Obama: . . . I think that we sort of hit a trough in September and October. Because up until that point, I think the feeling was that we were building an organization; we were raising money; we were in the hunt. . . . Right after Labor Day, you started seeing this big gap where Hillary started having a twenty point, twenty-five point lead. The press started getting in that cycle where each story feeds on itself, you know: "Why is this not working?" And people start trying to find explanations for why you're twenty-five points behind, which means you must be an idiot, and some people try to look for an explanation of all the things you've done wrong, and funders start getting nervous and supporters start getting nervous and making suggestions. And people are second-guessing themselves. So we got in one of those negative spirals. It probably reached its nadir in October.

Q: Was this when the fundraisers were grumbling?

Obama: Yeah, around that time, this is all roughly around the same time. And the truth was that at that point, I was actually pretty, I had grown . . . in a puzzling kind of way, I was growing more confident that we could win this thing because we had kept pace on the fundraising, because of the fact that in each successive debate, my performance had improved to the point where in the final four or five debates before Iowa, I felt that I was performing on a par with Hillary, even if the press didn't. I felt comfortable with how to communicate in these sound bites, which was not my strength. And because I always had a lot of confidence in our team in Iowa, we had a great organization, wonderful people, who had worked on the ground. The polls in Iowa were not twenty points apart. We felt that we had the best organization in Iowa, so in an odd way I was actually pretty calm.

It was during that period [when] I had that meeting with the fundraisers to give them an assurance that we are going to win this thing and everybody's gotta just stay calm. It was at that point where I did ask my team to pick up the pace. . . . We had gotten sluggish, and we had to push ourselves harder. It was at that point where I had to dig deeper and make sure that I was pushing hard. It was at that point where we also realized we were going to have to make our case more clearly, and more directly [explain] why I would be a better president than Hillary Clinton or John Edwards, as opposed to just talking about what I wanted to do and what my plans were for the country. [We realized that] I had to be very specific and say, "I should be president because I can bring the country together. I'm not subject to special interests. I think I will be straight with the American people, and that's what's needed."

Q: Now your team aside for a second . . .

Obama: . . . And by the way, that whole process built up to the JJ [Jefferson-Jackson] dinner, which I think was the real turning point in Iowa, and then the turning point of the campaign as a whole.

Q: What more did you ask of yourself at this point?

Obama: Well, you know, I think that . . . [*here Obama turned to look out of the window and fell silent for a full seventeen seconds*]. David Axelrod said something to me very early on, this was actually in the group meeting when we were deciding to run. And he said, "What I worry about most, Barack, about you running, is you may be too normal to win a presidential campaign." And I think what he meant—you can ask him what he meant—but I think what he meant was, I'm not . . . [*another pause, twelve seconds this time*] I'm not just . . . I've never felt that my worth is dependent on me winning this presidential campaign, that I have something that I have to prove. There was a time in my life where I had that feeling, because of an absent father, or always being a little bit of an outsider—you can psychoanalyze me and say, "Here's why he's a driven person." But I love my kids and I love my wife, and I love going to the movies without a fuss or reading a good book on a beach somewhere. . . . So there were from the start . . . some tensions in me about throwing myself into this and being consumed by it, and losing perspective, and losing touch with what were those things I believed were most important in life. I'm not trying to suggest that I'm some sort of reluctant candidate; obviously this is a choice I made. But there was some tension there in my own mind.

Q: Did you have to reconcile yourself with saying, "I'm going to have to spend more time away from my family?" Was that the crux of it?

Obama: Well, yeah, not only that, but I have to embrace this path that I've chosen, and not keep on thinking about the path that wasn't chosen. And, and, it was throwing yourself into it and not holding anything back, so I think it was more of a mindset than it was any particular [thing].

Q: Let me change tacks here a little bit. The law of inertia is a law for a reason and in a political campaign or I guess in any endeavor, particularly if things are going well, changing from the course that you're on is not the easy or natural thing to do. Given that you have defied everyone's expectations except maybe your own, as you move into the general . . . in terms of figuring out what you need to do better, about where you need to tighten things up, is that made more difficult by the fact that you all have done so well? Do you think you have a clear sense as a campaign . . .

Obama: No, no . . . I think that one thing I'm pretty good at is being my own best critic. Nobody's harder on me than me. I think that there are a lot of things that we need to do better, not just to win in November, but also to govern. I'm a firm believer that the habits you establish now carry over. If you're undisciplined now, you'll be undisciplined later. If there are areas of weakness in our organization now, that will reflect itself in my presence, and so . . . assuming we're successful in winning the nomination, we're going to have to do a lot of work to retool.

Q: Can you give me one or two examples of things you can do better?

Obama: . . . I think one of the things I said at the beginning of this campaign was that I wanted to block out a lot of time, especially early in the first two or three months of the campaign, to think about issues, because what I didn't want to do was just sort of paint by the numbers when it came to the policy side. I wanted to have conversations with the sharpest minds and the people who are pushing the envelope on health care or energy or education, to really drill down deep and figure out what is going to be . . . the menu of options that we have and what are those steps that are most likely to lead us, lead the country, in a better direction. And . . . not all that work was done, because the amount of time consumed just with politics, raising money, doing eight town hall meetings a day in Iowa, it just left very little time to devote to that kind of systematic, hard policy work. Now I think that our products, the policies we've offered are ones that I have great confidence in. And I think that our policy team has done a really good job, but my own involvement in us maybe stretching a little further and asking even tougher questions about what policies can really solve our energy crisis, for example, I'm not sure we've done that as well as we should have. . . . That was one of the tradeoffs of having to go from zero to sixty—we couldn't do everything exactly as well as we wanted to do. Now, potentially, we have a little more time to do it.

Q: Have you talked to Reverend Wright?

Obama: No.

Q: I understand that you were reluctant to even watch the video of him at the National Press Club, and I wonder if you can just take your mind back to when they handed you the transcript.

Obama: . . . My relationship with Reverend Wright and the church . . . and the fact that it became such an enormous issue, took me somewhat by surprise. Not entirely, but somewhat, first of all because it's a very conventional black church in a lot of ways. This whole thing about black liberation theology and black value system etc., etc., that's an overlay of some names that are given to very traditional aspects of the black church—preaching the social gospel, emphasizing your obligations to the community. Nine out of ten of Rev. Wright's sermons would stir no controversy whatsoever. He was not a public figure in Chicago beyond the church; he was not somebody like Jesse or Farrakhan who sought the public eye. He wasn't considered a firebrand. The church ministries are similar to church ministries all across the country. The membership is indistinguishable from the membership of most black churches.

I think that the first time that I got an inkling that this could be a problem was the day of the announcement, which has already been reported, where there was this article in *Rolling Stone* that my team showed to me that had some pretty incendiary language in it by Rev. Wright. The truth is that, like most busy people, I wasn't going to church every week, and he preaches three sermons a week. So particularly in the last two or three years, we hadn't been going that often, in part because I was campaigning and would be at other people's churches all the time. And what I understand from friends who are also members of the church was, after 9/11, Rev. Wright really ratcheted up some of the rhetoric, was a fierce critic of Bush, so some of his sermons became much more fiery. So I . . . that's when . . . when I [saw] that on the page, I thought to myself, "This doesn't sound real good." But my concern was not just the political ramifications; my concern was to figure out a way to protect the church from becoming a political issue. So that's the point where I called Rev. Wright, and I said, "You know what, you probably shouldn't introduce me, there's going to be 500 press credentials there, you don't want a whole bunch of mikes suddenly stuck in your face without any preparation or expectation." I know that that disappointed him, and I think he may have felt some anger about that.

Q: Did he express any?

Obama: I know it, and also [it's] what I heard from others . . . Shortly thereafter, there was an article by Jodi Kantor in *The New York Times* in which this was reported, and where [Wright] characterized our conversations. That put a further strain on the relationship because I didn't particularly appreciate him talking about a conversation that he and I had together, and suddenly it appearing in the *Times*. But my view at that point was that he was retiring, I had a strong commitment to the church community, he had gone through some very difficult times over the last several years, a number of his close friends had passed away, and the fact that he was retiring, [that] this is what he had built . . . his life of preaching, and now he was about to leave. So my instinct was to simply let him stay out of the limelight and to not make a bigger deal out of it. I was, that was, though, the first time I learned about the quote surrounding 9/11, it was in that *Times* article. And at that point I think both myself and my team anticipated that this will be a big problem at some point.

Fast forward, after Iowa, I don't know exactly when . . . [Sean] Hannity had played this up initially, his perspective on it was so ignorant, of black history, black traditions, black culture, black church. . . . His attempt to make this innocuous statement of the black value system [into] some statement of black separatism was so ludicrous that it didn't get a lot of traction, and we didn't expect it would. But, I'll be honest with you, this is an example of a failing, a shortcoming in our campaign. Immediately after that *New York Times* article came out, I, and a number of our senior folks, said to our research team, "Let's pull every single sermon that Rev. Wright's made, because it could be an issue, and it could be attributed to me, and let's at least know exactly what we're dealing with." That never got done. So that when the loop came, that did take us by surprise, packaged in that fashion, how offensive it was, I think [it] caught all of us off guard. I had just come back from Washington, [and] I had to immediately draft a statement. I had to appear that night on the cable shows to denounce the words but try to place them in some context, and it was that weekend that I prepared to write the race speech and was able then to deliver it in Philadelphia. And at that point, I don't think there was any question that this was going to be very damaging politically. On the other hand, I felt it was important to not disown somebody who I've known for a long time, who'd always treated me with great courtesy and kindness, and had treated my family very well, who was at the center of the church community that I valued, and who, for all his flaws, had done very good work. And that's what I tried to express in the speech, was this sense that people are complicated. They're a mixture of good and bad.

. . . I was shocked by a number of the things [Wright said]. I think the thing about AIDS was probably the most shocking, because that's classic sort of conspiracy theorizing in the African American community. It's not uncommon, but for somebody of Rev. Wright's education, it's not something that I would have expected. So I was very surprised by that. I did have a conversation with him after I delivered the speech in Philadelphia, and I told him in no uncertain terms how profoundly I disagreed with what he had to say, how offensive it was both to me and the American people, and I suggested to him that he needed to internalize and understand why people would be offended. And so, to see him then *not* process any of that, or engage in any self reflection, but to go out three consecutive days in an escalating fashion, culminating in a performance at the National Press Club that showed very little regard for the sensibilities of the American people, very little regard for my own sensibilities, that defended [the] indefensible statement, and that did so in a way that was often rude and mocking of people in the audience and in the viewing audience, was something very painful.

Q: You take a lot of pride in your roots as a community organizer, in being not far removed from the sort of everyday American experience. And I'm sure you know as well as anyone that there's no bubble quite like the presidency; there's nothing that insulates you from the rest of us like the presidency. Do you think much about this? Do you worry at all about this?

Obama: Absolutely. I worry about it all the time. I benefit from the fact that Michelle and her family are very rooted, and almost prototypical Americans, and [from] my friends—like Marty Nesbitt and Eric Whitaker and Valerie [Jarrett], or my friend who I just saw in Oregon, Greg Orme, who was traveling with me, my friend from high school who now works as a contractor—[from the fact that] most of my good friends are not in politics and are not in the political world. I feel that they help me stay tuned in to what's going on with people. But I do worry about it. More than anything what I worry about is the fact that I now change the atmosphere in any room that I walk into, or any conversation that I enter into. That people are going to speak to me differently now than they might have five years ago, even people whom I'm close to. That is something I worry about. And how to prevent that is going to be one of the most important challenges of the presidency.

ACKNOWLEDGMENTS

THE *Newsweek* PRESIDENTIAL election projects began in 1984, written by the greatest of *Newsweek* writers, Peter Goldman. In 1996, Peter turned over the writing duties to me, but he has stayed on to oversee the reporting, and he remains the heart and soul of this very long, very expensive quadrennial effort. In September of 2007, Peter began dispatching his team into the field: on the Democratic side, Daren Briscoe, Nick Summers and Eleanor Clift; and on the Republican side, Katie Connolly and Michael Hastings. After the field settled down (and Hastings left *Newsweek* in the spring of 2008), Katie became the permanent McCain correspondent, Daren covered Obama full-time (as he had from the beginning), and Nick followed Clinton, then later reported on Obama, Biden, and Palin. Eleanor, one of the best sourced reporters in Washington, covered both Obama and Clinton.

These reporters did an extraordinary job. The story told here was driven and largely shaped by their original reporting. When I detached from the magazine to join the project team at the end of August, I was as always counseled by Goldman and the editor on the project, Alexis Gelber, my colleague and friend of two decades. We were blessed to have a very resourceful, dedicated, and No Drama researcher, Daniel Stone, and two talented photo editors, Michelle Molloy and Elizabeth Johnson. A tip of the hat as well to a couple of *Newsweek* political reporters who chipped in key contributions: Holly Bailey and Jonathan Darman.

I am very grateful to the founder and editor-at-large of PublicAffairs, Peter Osnos, who saw the potential for this project-turned-book from the get-go, and to the book version's able editor, Lindsay Jones. At PublicAffairs, my thanks, too, to Clive Priddle, the editorial director; Melissa Raymond, the managing editor; Pete Garceau, the art director; and Susan Weinberg, the publisher.

At *Newsweek*, I want to thank the outgoing president and editor-in-chief, Rick Smith, whose faith in this most ambitious of journalistic endeavors was backed for many years by a virtually open checkbook; Donald Graham, the chairman of the Washington Post Company; and two essential supporters of the project, my close friends at *Newsweek*, managing director Ann McDaniel and the magazine's editor, Jon Meacham.

PUBLICAFFAIRS is a publishing house founded in 1997. It is a tribute to the standards, values, and flair of three persons who have served as mentors to countless reporters, writers, editors, and book people of all kinds, including me.

I. F. STONE, proprietor of *I. F. Stone's Weekly*, combined a commitment to the First Amendment with entrepreneurial zeal and reporting skill and became one of the great independent journalists in American history. At the age of eighty, Izzy published *The Trial of Socrates*, which was a national bestseller. He wrote the book after he taught himself ancient Greek.

BENJAMIN C. BRADLEE was for nearly thirty years the charismatic editorial leader of *The Washington Post*. It was Ben who gave the *Post* the range and courage to pursue such historic issues as Watergate. He supported his reporters with a tenacity that made them fearless, and it is no accident that so many became authors of influential, best-selling books.

ROBERT L. BERNSTEIN, the chief executive of Random House for more than a quarter century, guided one of the nation's premier publishing houses. Bob was personally responsible for many books of political dissent and argument that challenged tyranny around the globe. He is also the founder and was the longtime chair of Human Rights Watch, one of the most respected human rights organizations in the world.

⋅   ⋅   ⋅

For fifty years, the banner of Public Affairs Press was carried by its owner Morris B. Schnapper, who published Gandhi, Nasser, Toynbee, Truman, and about 1,500 other authors. In 1983 Schnapper was described by *The Washington Post* as "a redoubtable gadfly." His legacy will endure in the books to come.

Peter Osnos, *Founder and Editor-at-Large*